The Panic Instinct

The Behavioral Finance Reflex That Makes You Sell at the Worst Moment

Jordan Ellis

First edition, 2026

Published by Jordan Ellis

Contents

Contents

Foreword

I didn't set out to write a book about panic. I set out, a few years ago, to write about financial mistakes in general — the ordinary, well-documented ones: chasing returns, ignoring fees, holding on to a losing position out of stubbornness. Panic-selling was supposed to be one line item in a longer list. It refused to stay there.

Every person I talked to about their worst financial decision told nearly the same story, regardless of income, education, or how long they'd been investing. Not a story about bad math. A story about a moment — a red number, a phone call, a headline — after which they could no longer remember choosing anything. Their hand had already moved. The explanation came later, stitched together to make sense of an action that had already happened. I heard this from a woman who managed other people's money for a living and still sold her own account in under five minutes. I heard it from a man who could recite the statistics on market recovery from memory and sold anyway, the same afternoon he recited them to me.

That's the moment this book exists to name. Not the slow, background worry about money — that's a real subject, and it deserves its own careful treatment elsewhere. This is about the four seconds nobody plans for: the gap between a threat registering and a decision executing, a gap so narrow that most people never notice it exists until they're already on the other side of it, holding cash they didn't mean to be holding.

I have a stake in this because I don't think the standard advice works, and I think most people already suspect it doesn't. "Stay calm." "Don't panic." "Think long-term." None of it survives contact with an alarm that fires faster than thought. Telling someone not to panic in the moment of panicking is a bit like telling someone not to flinch — true in principle, useless in practice. What actually helps is understanding the machinery well enough to see it coming, and building something concrete in its path before the next alarm rings.

This book is that attempt. It doesn't promise you'll stop feeling the jolt. It only promises you'll finally know what it is — and that knowing changes what happens next.

Introduction

You have felt it before you could name it. A number moves the wrong way on a screen, and something in you moves before your thinking does — a tightening across the chest, a jolt down through the stomach, a hand already reaching for the phone before you've decided to reach for anything. By the time a coherent thought arrives — *maybe I should sell* — it doesn't feel like a thought at all. It feels like the only sane response to danger that's already arrived. You're not weighing a decision. You're getting out of the way of something that feels like it's bearing down on you, and the getting-out-of-the-way happens first, with the reasoning trailing behind it, doing the much smaller job of explaining a decision your body already made.

This book is about that moment, and only that moment. It is not about being generally afraid of losing money, or generally averse to risk, or generally pessimistic about the future — those are slower, quieter, background weather patterns, and other books cover them well. This is about something sharper and faster: the acute, event-triggered impulse to act — to sell, to flee, to liquidate, to get out — the instant a threat registers, even when the single best thing you could do is nothing at all. It is the difference between disliking rain and running for cover the second you feel the first drop, soaked or not, coat in hand or not, because some part of you has already decided that standing still in a downpour is unthinkable. Most people who panic-sell are not making a considered bet that prices will keep falling. They are fleeing, the way you'd flee a sound in the dark, and the flight itself is the whole event. The reasoning comes after, dressed up to look like it came first.

Consider two people, on two different afternoons, years apart, in situations that look nothing alike on paper. The first is a woman in her forties, sitting at her kitchen table with a laptop open to an account she built over fifteen years of steady contributions, watching a red number get redder across a single trading session. She has read enough, over the years, to know intellectually that broad downturns have always recovered given enough time, that her own plan was built with exactly this kind of week in mind, that the entire strategy she chose was chosen precisely so she wouldn't have to make emotional decisions on days like this one. None of that knowledge is present to her right now. What's present is a sensation she'd describe, if asked, as something between falling and drowning — the sense that the ground she was standing on has become the direction things are moving, and that standing still on moving ground is not a neutral choice but a dangerous one. She sells that afternoon. Not because she calculated that selling was correct. Because sitting there, watching the number fall, doing nothing had become physically unbearable, and selling was the only action available that made the unbearable feeling stop.

The second is a man in his late twenties, three years into a first serious attempt at investing, who wakes up to a headline about a company he's never heard of, in an industry adjacent to his own, and feels the floor of his understanding drop out from under him in about four seconds. He doesn't hold shares in the company. He holds a diversified position in something else entirely, chosen with reasonable care. But the headline does something specific to him: it makes an abstract, distant category of risk — *things can go wrong in ways I can't predict* — suddenly concrete, immediate, and personal, in a way it wasn't ninety seconds earlier when he was still asleep. He spends the next two hours reading everything he can find, not to gather information calmly, but the way you'd check every door and window after hearing a noise downstairs — not looking for facts so much as looking for permission to stop feeling this way. By mid-morning, he has sold the position that had nothing to do with the headline, because he could no longer tell the difference between a threat to that specific company and a threat to the entire idea that markets were a place his money could safely live. Neither of these people made a bad calculation. Both of them made no calculation at all. They responded to a threat, the way a body is built to respond to a threat, and the market happened to be where the threat showed up.

A third scene, quieter than the first two, belongs here as well, because the panic instinct doesn't only show up in dramatic single afternoons — sometimes it shows up as a long, slow erosion that only looks sudden from the outside. A retired couple, several years into drawing down the savings they spent three decades building, watch a prolonged downturn stretch from one difficult week into a difficult month. Nothing about their actual spending needs has changed. Nothing about the specific reason they built a diversified, professionally reviewed drawdown plan has changed either — the plan, in fact, was built with a stretch exactly like this one already priced into its assumptions. But somewhere around week three, something shifts in how they're relating to the number, not the number itself: the ongoing decline stops registering as market weather and starts registering as an emergency they are failing to respond to. They move a large portion of what remains into cash within a single afternoon, a decision neither of them can fully explain afterward except to say that they "couldn't just keep watching it happen." The event that finally triggered the flee response wasn't a single sharp drop. It was the accumulated weight of many small ones, crossing some threshold neither of them had consciously set, at which ongoing exposure to the falling number itself became the thing they could no longer tolerate.

A fourth scene rounds out the picture, because the panic instinct doesn't confine itself to people actively watching a number — sometimes it arrives secondhand, carried by someone else's fear before you've had any chance to form a read of your own. A young father, newly responsible for a small inherited account he hasn't paid much attention to since it landed in his name, gets a call from his brother-in-law, who has just sold everything in his own, unrelated portfolio and wants to talk about it. The brother-in-law isn't trying to alarm anyone; he's rattled, and he's talking the way rattled people talk — fast, certain, already three steps ahead of the actual facts. The young father hangs up forty minutes later having said very little and having checked nothing of his own, and yet something in him has already shifted: a diffuse, borrowed dread has settled where a neutral, unexamined afternoon used to sit. He opens his own account not because anything in it has changed, but because his brother-in-law's fear has become, for the moment, indistinguishable from his own. Within the week, without ever identifying a single concrete reason specific to his own holdings, he's sold too — not chasing evidence, but chasing the relief of no longer being the one person left on the call still holding something.

This is the pattern the whole book is built around, and it's worth being precise about what makes it different from the more familiar villain in most money psychology — loss aversion, the well-documented tendency to feel a loss more intensely than an equivalent gain. Loss aversion is a bias in how you *value* things: a dollar lost feels like more than a dollar, so you weigh potential losses more heavily than potential gains when you're choosing between options, sitting still, thinking it through. It is passive. It sits quietly in the background of every financial decision you make, coloring the math without necessarily forcing your hand. A person can carry a strong loss-aversion bias their entire life, hold it in the back of every decision they make, and never once panic-sell anything, because loss aversion by itself doesn't demand action — it only tilts the scale slightly whenever a decision is already being weighed. What this book is about is not that background coloring. It's the moment loss aversion stops being a bias in a calculation and becomes a trigger for action — the instant, involuntary lurch toward *doing something*, right now, regardless of whether the math has been done at all. You can carry loss aversion your whole life and never panic-sell a single position, if nothing ever forces the acute moment. And you can panic-sell despite knowing every relevant statistic, despite having built a plan specifically designed to survive this exact day, because knowing something and being able to act on it under a flood of threat-signal are two entirely different capacities, and only one of them is reliably online when the alarm goes off. Put plainly: loss aversion explains why a loss stings more than a gain feels good. It does not, by itself, explain why a person who deeply understands that fact still finds themselves selling everything in nine minutes flat. That second thing needs its own explanation, and that explanation is this book.

That's the real subject here: not what you believe about money, but what your body does the instant it decides money is under attack. And the reason this deserves its own book, rather than a chapter in a broader one, is that this reflex has its own separate machinery — older, faster, and largely indifferent to whatever careful financial education you've accumulated. The part of you that decides, calmly, over years, to build a diversified position and hold it through volatility is not the same part of you that, on one specific Tuesday, decides the only sane move is to get out immediately. They can coexist in the same person, hold contradictory views, and take turns running the show — and the second one, when it takes the wheel, does not consult the first one first. Understanding why requires understanding where the impulse actually comes from, which is where this book spends real time: not in finance, but in the much older architecture of threat response, built for a world with claws and cliffs and sudden shadows, now firing in response to a red number on a screen because that's the closest thing the modern world offers to what it was built to detect.

Here is the shape of the argument ahead, chapter by chapter, so you know what you're walking into. Each chapter isolates one specific trigger or mechanism inside this larger reflex — the visual jolt of a falling number, the pull of watching everyone else run, the story your mind manufactures to justify a decision it already made, the specific kind of speed that helps you dodge a car and hurts you in a downturn, the vertigo of not knowing where the bottom is, the relief that selling provides even when it's the wrong move, the expensive detour of buying back in after you've already sold low, and the way one panic event makes the next one easier to trigger. Each chapter follows you into a close, specific scene — sometimes two, from different corners of a financial life, because this reflex doesn't only live in stock portfolios; it lives in home sales during downturns, in retirement accounts during downturns, in small-business decisions during downturns, in any place where an asset's value moves visibly and a person is watching. Each chapter then names the real mechanism underneath — the actual, researched psychology, credited honestly, never invented for effect — counts what the pattern costs, and hands you concrete ways to interrupt it before it fires, or slow it down enough that the slower, wiser part of you gets a vote.

It's worth being honest, too, about the two people at the kitchen table and the headline that arrived at four in the morning, because their stories share a feature worth naming directly: neither of them was uninformed. The woman with the account she'd built over fifteen years had, by any reasonable measure, done the homework — she could have explained, calmly, on a normal Tuesday, exactly why downturns recover and why her plan was built to survive one. The young man reading the headline about a company he'd never held could have told you, the day before, that a single piece of bad news in an adjacent industry says nothing reliable about a diversified position built with entirely different holdings. Their information was not the problem. Their information was sitting exactly where it needed to be, fully intact, ready to be used — and it simply wasn't consulted, because the system that acted first doesn't route its decisions through the part of the brain where that information lives. This is the detail that makes the panic instinct so much harder to solve than ordinary financial ignorance: ignorance can be fixed by learning something new. This can't, because there's nothing new to learn. Both of them already knew it.

One master idea holds the whole book together, and you can carry it loosely until each chapter earns its share of it: the impulse to flee was never a flaw in your judgment about money. It's a completely intact, perfectly functional survival system, running exactly the way it was built to run, applied to a threat it was never designed to correctly assess. You are not bad at investing because you panic. You panic because you are, underneath the modern person who reads statements and rebalances portfolios, still carrying the same wiring that once needed to decide, in a fraction of a second and without a committee meeting, whether the shape in the grass was a threat worth running from. That wiring saved your ancestors' lives more times than anyone will ever be able to count. It is also, unmodified, catastrophically bad at telling the difference between a market correction and a predator, because it was never asked to make that distinction. No version of the environment that built this wiring ever contained a diversified retirement account, a thirty-year time horizon, or a number that could fall sharply on a Tuesday and fully recover by the following spring — none of the concepts this book spends its chapters on existed for the overwhelming majority of the time this system spent being built. It is not out of date in the way a piece of old advice is out of date. It is out of date the way a tool built for an entirely different job is out of date: still sharp, still fast, still working exactly as designed, simply pointed at something it was never meant to cut. It only had one job: decide fast, and decide toward safety. It still does that job today, with total confidence, in a context where the fastest decision is very often the worst one available.

This is not a book about being calmer in some general, aspirational sense, and it will not ask you to simply "not panic" — advice that has never once worked on anyone in the actual moment of panicking, because panic, by definition, is not a state you can reason your way out of using the same channel that produced it. What this book offers instead is narrower and more useful: a working map of exactly when and how the alarm fires, so you can recognize the specific moment it's happening — not after, in hindsight, but during, while there's still time to do something other than what the alarm is telling you to do. Every override in this book works the same way. None of them ask you to feel less afraid. All of them ask you to build a small delay, a small ritual, a small piece of pre-built structure between the alarm and the action — because the alarm cannot be silenced, but the gap between the alarm and the action can be widened, and that gap, it turns out, is nearly the entire difference between a life occasionally disrupted by fear and a life repeatedly wrecked by it.

Here is what this book will not do, because it matters to say plainly. It will not tell you which investments to hold, which accounts to open, or what allocation is correct for your situation — that's a conversation for a professional who knows your specific life, and no book, this one included, should pretend to replace that. It will not promise that following every override guarantees a better financial outcome; markets are genuinely uncertain, and sometimes the thing you were afraid of turns out to be real. What it will do is make sure that when you act — sell, hold, buy, walk away — you're acting from a decision, not a reflex wearing a decision's clothes. Those two things can look identical from the outside and produce completely different lives from the inside. This book is written to help you tell them apart, in the only moment that has ever mattered: not before the alarm rings, and not long after, but right in the middle of it, while the ground still feels like it's moving and some part of you is already reaching for the door.

It's worth pausing, too, on a question most readers arrive with, even if they haven't phrased it out loud: if this reflex is so old, so wired, so completely indifferent to what you know, is there any point in reading a book about it at all? The honest answer is yes, but not for the reason you might expect. You're not reading this to argue your way out of a reflex — arguing with an alarm has never once worked, on anyone, in the actual instant it's ringing. You're reading this to change your relationship to the *gap* around the reflex: the small window of time between the alarm firing and your hand actually moving, which turns out to be far more workable than the alarm itself. That gap is where every piece of advice in this book actually lives. It is narrow, and it closes fast, but it is real, and it can be widened with practice — not through insight alone, but through pre-built habits installed long before the day they're needed. That's the entire promise of what follows: not a calmer nervous system, but a wider gap. It's worth being honest about what widening that gap will and won't feel like from the inside, because expectations matter for whether you stick with any of this past the first difficult week. It will not feel like the alarm getting quieter — for most people, the alarm's volume barely changes no matter how much practice they put in. What changes is what happens in the half-second, and then the minute, and then the hour after the alarm fires: whether a pre-built rule catches you before your hand finishes moving, or whether nothing does. Widening the gap is not the same project as calming down, and mistaking one for the other is the single most common reason people give up on this kind of work too early, concluding it “isn’t working” because they still felt the jolt as sharply as ever, without noticing that the jolt no longer got the last word.

It helps, before moving on, to say a word about what “wired-in” actually means here, because the phrase can sound like an excuse if it’s misread. It is not a claim that you’re powerless, and it is not a diagnosis. It’s closer to an anatomical fact, the same kind of fact as having a pulse or a startle reflex — true of every reader of this book, true regardless of income, education, or how many years of investing experience someone carries. A person with three advanced degrees in finance has the identical amygdala, running the identical fast circuitry, as a person who has never opened an account. Expertise changes what you know. It does not change how fast the alarm fires, and it is worth sitting with that asymmetry for a moment, because so much financial education implicitly assumes the opposite — that more knowledge produces more composure, in a straight line, forever. It doesn’t. Knowledge and composure are stored in different systems, built on different timelines, running at different speeds, and this book exists specifically in the gap between them.

One more note before the chapters begin, because it will save confusion later: you'll notice that each chapter follows the identical structure — a close scene or two, a mechanism section naming real, credited research, a costs section, and a set of overrides ending in one memorable line. This isn't accidental repetition. It's deliberate, because the whole argument of the book is that the panic instinct itself is repetitive — the same underlying event, dressed in a new trigger each time — and a book that kept changing its own shape to match each chapter's specific flavor would undercut the very point it's making. The structure is the argument. By the time you reach the last chapter, the shape itself should feel as familiar and recognizable as the alarm it's describing.

Let's start where the alarm itself starts — not in your portfolio, but in the much older room of the brain where every version of "get out now" has always been decided.

Chapter 1 — The Alarm That Doesn't Check the Calendar

Where the Flee Reflex Comes From, and Why It Can't Tell a Market From a Predator

Somewhere behind your eyes, roughly the size and shape of an almond, sits a piece of tissue that has never once seen a stock chart, never learned what a portfolio is, and does not know what a year is, let alone which one it's currently living through. It doesn't need to know any of that to do its job. Its job — the amygdala's job, to use the actual name — is to answer one question, over and over, thousands of times a day, faster than conscious thought can intervene: *is this a threat?* When the answer is yes, it doesn't wait for permission. It fires a cascade: a flood of stress hormones, a spike in heart rate, a narrowing of attention onto the threat and away from almost everything else. All of it is designed to get you moving before you've finished thinking about whether moving is a good idea. This system evolved across an almost incomprehensibly long stretch of time, in a world where the cost of a false alarm was mild — you ran from a shadow that turned out to be nothing, wasted thirty seconds, felt a little foolish — and the cost of a missed alarm was your life. Given that asymmetry, evolution did not build a system optimized for accuracy. It built a system optimized for speed, and it built that system to err, whenever there was any doubt at all, on the side of *run*.

This chapter is where the book explains that system honestly — not as a metaphor borrowed loosely from psychology to make a finance book sound more scientific, but as the actual, literal machinery your body deploys the moment your portfolio drops fast enough to register as a threat. Understanding it isn't a detour before the real content starts. It is the real content, because every chapter that follows is really just this same mechanism, viewed from a different angle, wearing a different specific trigger. Once you understand the alarm itself, the rest of the book becomes far less mysterious — you'll start to recognize the same signature in each new scene: something registers as danger, the body moves before the mind finishes its sentence, and the sentence, once it does finish, mostly exists to explain a decision that was already made.

Picture a woman standing at the edge of a hiking trail, years before any of this had anything to do with money, when a shape in the underbrush moves in a way that doesn't match the wind. She doesn't consciously reason through the possibilities — snake, branch, animal, nothing — and select the correct response. Her body has already jumped back, heart already hammering, breath already caught, a full second or more before any of that reasoning could have completed. If you asked her, right after, why she jumped, she'd tell you a story: *I saw movement and thought it might be a snake.* That story is true, in the sense that it accurately describes what she now believes happened. It is also, in a stricter sense, backwards — the jump came first, produced by a threat-detection system operating well below conscious awareness, and the tidy sentence about snakes was assembled afterward, by a different part of the brain entirely, to explain a decision that had already been executed. This is not a flaw in her. It's the system working exactly as designed: detect first, explain later, and make sure "later" is fast enough that you never notice the gap.

Now picture the same woman, a decade later, at her kitchen table, watching a retirement account lose more value in a single afternoon than she typically saves in half a year. The shape in the underbrush is gone. In its place is a number on a screen, changing color, moving in a direction that her body has already learned, from an entire lifetime of experience with falling things, correlates with danger. Her amygdala does not know the difference between a portfolio and a cliff edge. It was never built to know the difference — it evolved to respond to loss, to sudden negative change, to anything that reads as *the situation is getting worse and the ground beneath you is not stable*, using a template built long before markets existed. The red number gets processed through the exact same threat-detection pathway as the shape in the underbrush, because it is, structurally, the same kind of input: fast, negative, uncertain, and demanding an immediate response. Her heart rate rises. Her attention narrows to the screen, to the number, to the feeling of the ground moving — the identical physiological signature as the trail, just without the trail. And her hand moves toward the phone to call her advisor, or toward the app to sell, before she has consciously decided that selling is the correct financial move. It doesn't feel like a financial move at all in that moment. It feels like getting off the trail before the shape in the underbrush becomes something worse.

A second scene widens the picture beyond the kitchen table, because the alarm doesn't only fire for people watching an established, long-held account — it fires just as readily for someone with almost no financial history at all, which tells you something important about what actually triggers it. A college student, two months into a small, automated savings habit he's genuinely proud of, checks the app on a whim between classes and sees a number smaller than the one he remembers from a few days earlier — a modest, unremarkable dip, the kind of movement that means essentially nothing over any meaningful timeframe. He has no fifteen years of history to draw calm from, no plan document to point to, nothing except a vague, secondhand sense that "the market goes up over time." None of that matters in the moment. His hand is already moving to pause the automated contribution before he's formed a single coherent thought about why. What this scene adds to the first one is important: the alarm doesn't require a large account, a long history, or even real financial stakes to fire at full strength. It requires only a visible, negative, sudden-feeling change — the amygdala doesn't scale its response to the actual dollar amount at risk, because dollar amounts aren't the kind of information it evolved to process at all. It responds to the shape of the drop, identically, whether the account holds a few hundred dollars or a few hundred thousand.

Here is the deeper piece of the mechanism, and it's the part most people never get told plainly enough to actually use: the amygdala operates on a much faster circuit than the parts of your brain responsible for careful, weighed reasoning. Neuroscientist Joseph LeDoux, whose research mapped much of this threat-response architecture, described what's sometimes called the "low road" — a fast, crude pathway that sends sensory information almost directly to the amygdala, bypassing the slower, more accurate "high road" that runs the information through the cortex first, where it could be properly analyzed, contextualized, and weighed against everything else you know. The low road is faster and dumber. It reacts to a rough, blurry approximation of the input — enough to tell "possible threat" from "definitely fine," but not enough to distinguish "market correction inside a diversified thirty-year plan" from "everything is being taken from me right now." By the time the high road finishes its slower, more accurate analysis and arrives at something closer to the truth, the low road has often already made you move. This isn't a design flaw. It's a deliberate tradeoff, built by a process that had no way of knowing markets would ever exist, optimized entirely for a world where the extra half-second of accurate analysis was, often enough, the difference between surviving and not.

There's a further wrinkle in LeDoux's research worth understanding, because it explains why the low road doesn't just win the initial race but keeps winning long after the high road has caught up with better information. The amygdala doesn't simply forward a rough signal and step aside once the cortex takes over. It maintains an active, ongoing influence over attention itself — narrowing what you notice, tilting which details jump out at you, favoring anything that confirms danger over anything that would complicate the threat picture. This means the high road, even once it arrives, is not working from a neutral, complete set of facts. It's working from whatever the low road has already filtered and handed it, which is precisely why a person in the grip of financial panic can read an entire balanced analysis and walk away remembering only the one alarming sentence in it. The high road isn't slower and equally objective. It's slower and already working with tainted evidence, evidence the low road pre-selected on its way past.

This is also why willpower alone has never been a reliable defense against panic, and why so much financial advice that boils down to "just don't panic" fails so completely in the actual moment. Willpower is a high-road function — it lives in the slower, more deliberate parts of the brain, the same regions responsible for weighing evidence and planning ahead. The low road doesn't answer to it. By the time your slower, wiser reasoning arrives at the scene, the low road has often already fired the alarm, released the stress hormones, and started your hand moving toward the sell button — and asking the high road to overrule a decision that's already partially executed is a much harder job than asking it to make the decision in the first place. This is the honest reason panic-selling keeps happening to smart, informed, well-prepared people: intelligence and preparation are both high-road resources, and the moment that matters most is frequently decided before the high road even gets a seat at the table.

There's a second piece of the machinery worth understanding plainly, because it explains why the feeling doesn't just spike and fade the way a single startled jump does — why a bad financial afternoon can leave you keyed up for hours afterward, unable to settle, checking the number again and again long after the initial jolt has passed. The amygdala's threat signal doesn't act alone. It triggers a broader physiological cascade, running through what's sometimes called the hypothalamic-pituitary-adrenal axis, that releases stress hormones — adrenaline first, for the immediate spike, and cortisol close behind it, for the sustained elevation — designed to keep the whole body primed for continued action over a period of minutes to hours, not just the first half-second. This made excellent sense for the kind of threat the system evolved to handle: a predator encounter rarely resolved in one heartbeat, and staying physiologically primed for a while afterward — heart rate elevated, attention still narrowed, ready to run again if the threat returned — was often the difference between a close call and a second, fatal one. Applied to a market downturn, the same prolonged priming means the alarm doesn't switch off the moment you close the app. It lingers, chemically, for a stretch of real time, which is exactly why so many panic-driven financial decisions don't happen in the first four seconds but in the following hour or two — a second, third, or fourth decision, made while the body is still chemically primed from the first one, each one a little easier to justify than it would have been in a genuinely calm state.

This is also the piece of the mechanism that explains why the same event can trigger wildly different intensities of response in two otherwise similar people, and why that difference has very little to do with how much either of them actually understands about markets. The threshold at which this whole cascade fires isn't fixed identically across every nervous system — it's shaped by a person's individual history, their baseline stress load at the moment the trigger arrives, and, as later chapters will explore in detail, by whatever similar alarms have fired before and left a strengthened pathway behind them. Two people can look at the identical falling number, on the identical day, with the identical underlying financial plan, and one will feel a mild, manageable unease while the other experiences the full cascade — narrowed attention, racing heart, an overwhelming pull toward action — not because one of them is weaker or less disciplined, but because their two nervous systems arrived at that moment carrying different histories, different baseline loads, and different thresholds for what counts as dangerous enough to answer with the full response.

There's a related piece of research worth bringing in here, because it explains something the trail scene and the kitchen-table scene share that isn't fully covered by LeDoux's fast-and-slow pathway alone: why the body's signal shows up before any conscious content does, and why that signal itself functions as a kind of pre-verbal judgment rather than a neutral physical afterthought. The neuroscientist Antonio Damasio, studying patients with damage to specific areas of the brain responsible for integrating emotional and bodily signals into decision-making, developed what's known as the somatic marker hypothesis — the finding that ordinary, healthy decision-making relies heavily on bodily, felt signals (a tightening, a lightness, a sense of dread or ease) that get attached to possible outcomes before conscious reasoning ever evaluates them explicitly. These "somatic markers" function as a fast, embodied shortcut, letting you feel that an option is bad before you've worked out exactly why. Damasio's patients, whose brain damage disconnected this bodily signaling from their decision-making, didn't become more rational as a result. They became strikingly worse at ordinary decisions, endlessly deliberating over trivial choices, because the felt sense that normally narrows the field — this direction feels wrong, that one feels workable — was no longer available to guide them. The lesson cuts in an important, easily missed direction: the somatic markers that make ordinary daily decisions fast and workable are the identical machinery that makes the kitchen-table jolt so overwhelming. It's the same system, functioning perfectly, just firing on a target — a red number — it has no reliable basis for judging accurately. You cannot select which decisions the body weighs in on and which it stays silent for. It weighs in on all of them, market crashes and lunch orders alike, and the work of this book is not to quiet that voice but to stop mistaking its volume for its accuracy.

There's one more piece of the underlying biology worth naming plainly, because it clears up a common misunderstanding that keeps people from taking their own reactions seriously. Many people, on some level, believe their panic is "just in their head" — a mental event, an overreaction, something they should simply be able to think their way past if they tried a little harder. The research doesn't support that framing. The cascade this chapter describes is measurably physical: elevated cortisol, elevated heart rate, narrowed blood flow to peripheral reasoning, a body genuinely, chemically prepared for a fight-or-flight event that isn't actually happening. Telling yourself to "just calm down" during that cascade is a bit like telling a sprinter mid-race to simply stop being out of breath. The breathlessness isn't a mental habit. It's the direct physiological consequence of what the body is already doing. Financial panic works the same way — which is exactly why every override worth trusting in this book targets behavior and timing, not willpower or mood.

None of this means you're at the mercy of the low road forever, and that's the hopeful half of this chapter, worth sitting with before the harder material ahead. The low road is fast, but it isn't unreachable — it can be trained, the way a startle reflex can be dampened with repeated safe exposure, the way a soldier's instinctive flinch at a loud noise softens over years back in a quiet life. You cannot delete the alarm. You were not built with an off switch, and wanting one is like wanting to not need a heartbeat — understandable, but not on offer. What you can build, deliberately and with practice, is the gap between the alarm and the action: a beat of space where the low road has fired but the high road gets a chance to weigh in before anything irreversible happens. Every override in every chapter of this book is, underneath its specific wording, an attempt to build exactly that gap. None of them try to silence the amygdala. All of them try to slow down the distance between its signal and your hand.

It's worth naming, too, why this reflex deserves its own book rather than a chapter inside a broader study of financial fear, because the distinction matters for how you'll use everything ahead. General financial anxiety — a background hum of worry about not having enough, about the future being uncertain, about money never quite stretching far enough — is a real and separate problem, and it behaves differently. It's chronic rather than acute, diffuse rather than triggered by a specific event, and it responds to different tools: budgeting, reframing, building genuine security over time. The panic instinct is not that. It is narrow, sudden, and triggered — it needs an event, a visible drop, a headline, a conversation with someone else who is also afraid, something specific that crosses a threshold and flips the switch from background worry into foreground alarm. You can be a calm, financially secure person with no chronic money anxiety at all and still panic-sell the instant the right trigger arrives, because the trigger, not your baseline temperament, is doing most of the work. This book is a map of those triggers, one chapter at a time, so you can recognize each one on approach rather than only in the rearview mirror.

Here's what's ahead, briefly, so you can see the shape of the whole argument before the first close-up scene begins. Chapter 2 looks at the raw sensory jolt — the specific, almost pre-verbal reaction to a falling number or a red chart, and why the visual alone can trigger flight before any actual analysis has occurred. Chapter 3 turns to what happens when you're not alone in the panic — the pull of watching other people flee, and why a crowd moving toward the exits is one of the most powerful threat signals a human brain can receive, powerful enough to override your own independent judgment entirely. Chapter 4 examines the story your mind builds after the decision to flee has already been made — the confident, articulate narrative that arrives just in time to explain a choice that was never actually reasoned through. Chapter 5 looks directly at the speed itself: why the same fast-thinking system that saves you from a swerving car actively sabotages you in a slower-moving, statistically different kind of danger. Chapter 6 sits inside the specific vertigo of not knowing where the bottom is — the particular kind of fear that comes from open-ended uncertainty rather than a known, bounded loss. Chapter 7 names the relief that selling provides, in the moment, regardless of whether it was the right call — because action itself, not correctness, is often what the nervous system is actually seeking. Chapter 8 follows what happens after: the expensive detour of buying back in once the fear has passed, often at a worse price than the one you fled. And Chapter 9 closes the pattern by looking at what one panic event does to the next one — how fleeing once makes fleeing again easier, unless something is deliberately done to interrupt that trend.

By the end, you won't have a system that prevents fear. No such system exists, and any book that promises you one is selling something other than the truth. What you'll have instead is something more durable: a working, specific vocabulary for the exact moment fear turns into action, so that the next time the ground seems to move beneath a number on a screen, some small, trained part of you recognizes the shape of what's happening — not a cliff, not a predator, just the oldest alarm you own, firing at the closest thing the modern world has ever offered it to fire at.

One final piece of framing belongs here, before the book moves into its close-up chapters, because it will keep the rest of the material from landing as a list of disconnected symptoms rather than one coherent system. Every chapter ahead names a different doorway into the same room — different triggers (a color, a crowd, a story, a speed, an open question, a relief, a return, a repetition) all leading to the identical underlying event this chapter has just described: the low road firing before the high road arrives, a body moving before a mind finishes its sentence. You do not need to memorize eight separate problems. You need to recognize one problem, wearing eight different faces, and get comfortable enough with the shape of the first face — the one this chapter just described — that the other seven become easy to spot by family resemblance rather than by starting from scratch each time.

Let's start with the moment the alarm actually goes off — not the worry before it, not the regret after it, but the half-second the color changes and something in you decides, before you do, to run.

Chapter 2 — The Red Screen

Why a Falling Number Triggers Flight Before You've Finished Reading It

He doesn't remember deciding to open the app. His thumb is just there, on the icon, and then the screen is loading, and then it's red — not a specific number yet, not a specific loss, just a wash of red across a chart he's looked at a hundred times before in green. The red arrives roughly half a second before the number does, and in that half-second, before he's read a single digit, before he knows how much is actually gone, his stomach has already dropped. Something in him has already responded to the color alone. The number, when it finally resolves — a meaningful drop, though nowhere near catastrophic, nowhere near the kind of loss that would actually threaten anything he's built — barely changes what he's already feeling, because the feeling arrived before the number did. He sits with the phone in his hand for exactly four seconds before he starts scrolling toward the sell screen, and in none of those four seconds does he consciously think the sentence *I should sell this.* He just moves toward it, the way you'd move your hand off a stove before you'd finished registering the word "hot."

This is the pattern the whole chapter is built around: not the decision to sell, but the sensory jolt that arrives before any decision has had time to form, and how much of what follows is really just that jolt, dressed up afterward in the language of reasoning. The red screen isn't information yet when it hits you. It's closer to a physical event — a flash, a color, a shape of motion — processed by the same fast, crude system that would react to a sudden movement in your peripheral vision, before the slower, careful parts of your brain have even started reading. By the time you've actually parsed the number, your body may have already begun preparing to act on a threat you haven't consciously identified yet.

Consider a very different scene, involving no phone at all. A couple in their sixties, a few years from the retirement date they've been planning toward for over a decade, sit in a realtor's office reviewing an appraisal on the house they're selling as part of that plan — a house whose value, according to the appraisal, has come in meaningfully below what they'd assumed, below what they need it to be worth for the numbers in their retirement plan to work the way they'd assumed they would. There's no red chart here, no flashing screen. But the husband, reading the figure at the bottom of the page, feels something almost identical to what the young man felt looking at his portfolio: a fast, physical drop, arriving before he's finished doing the actual math on what this figure means for their timeline. He doesn't wait to run that math. Within the week, he's pushing to list the house immediately, below what the realtor thinks is a fair asking price, because some part of him has decided that the number on the page is a countdown, and that every day the house sits unlisted is a day of further, ongoing loss — a belief that isn't actually supported by anything in the appraisal, which measured a moment, not a trend. The jolt from reading one disappointing figure has translated directly into urgency to act, immediately, on incomplete information, in a domain — real estate, not day-trading — where speed is almost never the asset it feels like in the moment.

What connects the phone and the appraisal is not the asset class. It's the shape of the trigger: a piece of visual or textual information that reads, at a pre-verbal level, as *loss, now, getting worse* — and the body's response to that shape doesn't particularly care whether the underlying situation is actually urgent. It responds to the shape of the information, not its substance, and it responds faster than substance can be assessed.

A third scene shows the same jolt firing off something that isn't even a number. A small-business owner, checking a dashboard that tracks daily sales against a rolling average, watches the day's bar render shorter than yesterday's — a completely ordinary, statistically unremarkable fluctuation of the kind that happens dozens of times a year in any real business. But the bar renders in a muted gray rather than the usual blue, a formatting quirk of the software meant only to flag days below the rolling average, with no further meaning attached. He doesn't read it that way. The visual break from the pattern he's used to seeing — blue, blue, blue, then suddenly not — produces the identical fast drop the red chart produces in a portfolio app, and he spends the next twenty minutes drafting an email to his small staff about "tightening things up," a message he'll quietly delete an hour later once the following day's numbers come in perfectly normal. The jolt didn't need a falling number at all. It only needed a visual pattern-break that read, for half a second, as *something is wrong here.*

A second scene shifts the trigger from a screen to a mailbox, useful because it strips away the live, color-coded chart entirely and still produces the identical jolt. A woman in her fifties opens a quarterly retirement statement — plain paper, black ink, no red anywhere on the page — and finds the total on the front page smaller than the one she remembers from the last statement. There's no animation, no flashing color, nothing designed to alarm her. And yet the reaction arrives at the same speed as it would on a live app: a fast drop in her stomach, a tightening in her jaw, a full second or more before she's actually located the specific number that changed or done any arithmetic on how large the change actually was. She calls her plan provider that same afternoon to ask about moving to something "more conservative," a call she makes before she's compared this quarter's number to the number from two years earlier, which would have shown her a very different, far calmer picture. What this scene demonstrates is that the red screen isn't really about red, or even about screens — the underlying trigger is any format that delivers a negative number as a sudden, standalone fact, without the context that would let you judge it properly. A quarterly paper statement can do this exactly as effectively as a live chart, because the jolt was never coming from the pixels. It was coming from the shape of the information: bad news, delivered flat, with no immediate frame of reference attached.

What's actually happening

The psychologist Robert Zajonc spent much of his career studying something he called affective primacy — the finding, replicated many times since, that emotional reactions to a stimulus can occur before, and independently of, any conscious cognitive processing of what that stimulus actually is. His research suggested that the brain doesn't need to fully identify and analyze something before generating a feeling about it; a fast, low-resolution "gist" reaction can arrive first, and often arrives so quickly that it shapes — sometimes fully determines — the more deliberate judgment that follows, rather than the other way around. Applied to the red screen: your emotional system doesn't need to read the number to react to the color, the shape of the downward line, the general sense of "this looks bad." It reacts to that gist immediately, and the number you read a half-second later gets interpreted through the lens of a feeling that's already formed, rather than generating that feeling fresh from a neutral read of the actual figure.

This connects to what behavioral economists sometimes call the affect heuristic — a concept developed and studied extensively by researchers including Paul Slovic, working in the tradition Daniel Kahneman and Amos Tversky established with their broader research on judgment under uncertainty. The affect heuristic describes how people frequently substitute an easier question — "how does this make me feel?" — for a harder one — "what does the evidence actually suggest I should do?" — without realizing the substitution has happened. It feels, from the inside, like you're evaluating the situation. What you're actually doing, much of the time, is consulting a feeling that arrived before the evaluation started, and then reverse-engineering reasons that match it. The red screen generates the feeling almost instantly. The feeling then quietly directs which facts you go looking for next — usually facts that confirm the danger the feeling has already announced, because that's what a threat-response system is built to do: look for more evidence of the threat it's already detected, not evidence that might contradict it.

There's a reason color specifically carries this much weight, and it isn't arbitrary or purely cultural, though culture reinforces it. Red is used, across an enormous range of contexts — warning labels, stop signs, emergency lighting, blood — as a near-universal signal of danger or urgency, and repeated exposure to that pairing strengthens an association that likely has some root in more basic biology as well, given red's long-standing connection to visible injury and exposed tissue. Financial software didn't invent this association; it borrowed an association your nervous system had already built, for entirely different reasons, over an entire lifetime of encountering red as a marker of "pay attention, something is wrong." When a portfolio app renders a loss in red, it isn't neutrally displaying data. It's activating a pre-existing alarm circuit, and doing so before you've had any chance to evaluate whether the specific loss shown actually warrants alarm.

The couple in the realtor's office experienced a version of the same thing without any color at all — proof that the trigger isn't really about red pixels specifically, but about the shape of the information landing as *sudden, negative, and requiring an answer right now.* A number on a page, delivered in a moment already charged with anxiety about an approaching deadline, can generate the identical fast, pre-verbal drop that a red chart generates, because the nervous system isn't actually parsing "portfolio" versus "house appraisal." It's parsing "bad news just arrived, and it feels urgent," and that parsing happens at a speed that has nothing to do with which asset class is technically involved.

Zajonc's research also identified something worth naming specifically here: the affective reaction doesn't just arrive first, it tends to be remembered more vividly and for longer than the factual content that followed it. In studies of how people recall emotionally charged information, the feeling attached to an event frequently outlasts the specific details that produced it — people forget the exact figures, the exact wording of a headline, the exact percentage a chart showed, while the general feeling of alarm persists intact, sometimes for years. This is part of why a single bad red-screen afternoon can leave a lasting imprint on how someone relates to checking their accounts, long after the specific numbers involved have become impossible to recall accurately. The feeling was never really about that specific number to begin with. It was about the shape and color of the moment, and shapes and colors are exactly what the memory holds onto most stubbornly.

It's worth being precise about the actual sequence involved, because knowing the sequence is most of what makes it interruptible. First, a sensory input arrives — a color, a shape of motion, a number's general size and direction — processed at a resolution too crude to distinguish "mild" from "severe," only "bad" from "not bad." Second, the affective system generates a feeling matched to that crude read, not to the actual, specific severity of the situation, because the specific severity hasn't been assessed yet and won't be for another second or two. Third — and this is the step most people never notice happening at all — the feeling itself becomes the input the rest of your thinking responds to, rather than the original information. By the time you consciously register the actual number, you're not evaluating it fresh. You're evaluating it through a feeling that arrived a half-second earlier and has already started shaping what you notice, what you search for, and what conclusion feels obviously correct. This is why two people can look at the identical figure and walk away with opposite readings of how serious it is: they're not disagreeing about the number. They're each interpreting it through a different feeling that arrived before either of them finished reading it.

There's a further layer worth adding here, drawn from research on the neuroscience of fear learning conducted by Elizabeth Phelps and colleagues, which examined how quickly the human brain can register an emotionally significant image — even one flashed too briefly to consciously perceive — and still produce a measurable physiological fear response. Her work demonstrated that emotionally charged visual stimuli can trigger amygdala activation and downstream physiological changes at speeds well below the threshold of conscious recognition, meaning the brain can register "threat" from a shape or color before the viewer could report having seen anything specific at all. This matters directly for the red screen: it isn't a coincidence, or an exaggeration, that the man on the couch felt his stomach drop before he'd read the number. Phelps's research suggests the wash of red itself may be registering as an emotionally significant signal at a genuinely subliminal speed, faster than the half-second he might guess it took, faster than any account of "reading the chart" can actually describe. You are not slow to notice the number. The number was never what you noticed first.

What it costs you

The most direct cost is the one that shows up in account statements: decisions made in the four seconds after the jolt, before any actual analysis has occurred, are decisions made with the least information you will ever have about the situation. The young man selling four seconds after a color change doesn't know whether the drop reflects a genuine structural problem, a brief overreaction, or simple day-to-day volatility inside a plan built to expect exactly this. He's not choosing based on that distinction. He's choosing based on the speed of the color change relative to the speed of his own capacity to think, and the color always wins that race, because it was never a fair race to begin with — one side has millions of years of head start.

The quieter cost is what this does to your relationship with the information itself. Every time a jolt precedes and overrides a considered decision, the association between "checking my accounts" and "danger incoming" gets reinforced a little further, which makes the next check harder, and the jolt on the next check a little sharper. This is how people end up avoiding their own financial information entirely — not from laziness, but because checking has been repeatedly paired, in their own nervous system, with an unpleasant, involuntary physical event. The habit of looking becomes the habit of bracing, and eventually people simply stop looking, which creates an entirely separate set of problems this book's sister volumes address. The panic reflex and the avoidance reflex are, in this sense, cousins — one runs toward frantic action, the other runs toward not looking at all, and both are downstream of the same overwhelming, pre-verbal jolt.

There's a third cost worth naming specifically, because it compounds quietly over a lifetime rather than showing up in any single decision: the more times a jolt is allowed to run the show uninterrupted, the more confident the pathway producing it becomes, and the harder it becomes, later, to trust your own read of any financial information at all — good news included. A person who has learned, through repetition, that their gut reaction to a falling number is unreliable often starts distrusting their gut reaction to a rising one too, second-guessing genuine opportunities and genuine reasons for confidence with the same reflexive suspicion they've learned to apply to panic. The jolt doesn't just cost you in the moment it fires. Left unexamined, it slowly erodes your ability to trust any fast financial instinct, including the ones that were actually right.

There's a fourth cost worth naming, one that shows up specifically in households and partnerships rather than in any single person's account. When one partner is prone to the jolt and the other isn't, or when the two people involved are prone to it on different timelines, the mismatch itself becomes a recurring source of friction that has nothing to do with either person's actual financial judgment. One partner reads the red screen and needs to act; the other reads the same screen and feels nothing urgent at all, and each interprets the other's reaction as the wrong one — reckless on one side, unfeeling on the other — when in fact both are simply reporting an honest, involuntary physiological response that happened to fire at different intensities in two different nervous systems looking at the same number. Left unnamed, this becomes a recurring argument dressed up as a disagreement about money, when it's really a disagreement about two different jolt thresholds meeting the same red screen.

The overrides

Separate the color from the number, deliberately, every time. Before you read any figure — a balance, a chart, a change percentage — pause long enough to notice the jolt happening, and name it silently: *that's the color, not the number yet.* This sounds almost too small to matter, but it works by inserting a half-second of conscious noticing into a process that otherwise runs entirely below awareness. You cannot stop the affective primacy response from firing. You can catch it firing, which is the necessary first step to keeping it from steering the rest of the decision.

The Move: build a mandatory delay between the jolt and any irreversible action. Choose a specific number now, while you're calm, and commit to it: no selling, no listing, no liquidating anything within a fixed window — twenty-four hours is a reasonable standard — of any moment that produced a strong physical reaction. Write this rule down somewhere you'll actually see it again, before you need it, because you will not be able to construct a sensible rule in the moment the jolt hits; the whole point of the rule is that it's built by the calmer version of you, in advance, for the benefit of the version of you who won't be capable of calm reasoning when it matters. This is the single highest-leverage override in this chapter, because it doesn't ask you to feel differently — it only asks you to act on a delay, which is a behavior, not a feeling, and behaviors can be pre-committed to in a way feelings cannot.

Change how the information is delivered to reduce the raw sensory hit. If a specific visual format — a live, color-coded, real-time chart — reliably produces the jolt, consider checking your position through a plainer, less visually charged format: a written statement, a flat number without the color-coded chrome, viewed on a schedule you choose rather than a feed you're exposed to continuously. This isn't about avoiding information. It's about receiving the same information through a channel less optimized to trigger the pre-verbal alarm before the slower, more accurate parts of your thinking get a chance to engage.

Rehearse the four seconds before you need them. In a calm moment, imagine the red screen appearing, vividly, and imagine yourself noticing the jolt, naming it, and waiting instead of acting. This isn't a magic fix — a single mental rehearsal won't erase millions of years of wiring — but repeated rehearsal of a specific response, done consistently, is one of the few things with actual evidence behind it for changing how quickly a trained response can compete with an automatic one. You are, in effect, giving your slower brain a head start it wouldn't otherwise have.

Ask what the feeling arrived before you'd read, specifically, before trusting its verdict. Once you notice a strong reaction to a piece of financial information, ask directly: what did I actually finish reading before this feeling showed up?

Often the honest answer is “almost nothing” — a color, a headline’s first few words, a shape on a chart — which makes it much easier to recognize that the feeling was responding to a crude gist, not to the actual content, and doesn’t yet deserve the authority it’s claiming.

If you share financial decisions with someone else, name the jolt-mismatch explicitly, before it becomes an argument about something else. If you and a partner, co-owner, or family member tend to react to the same financial information at different speeds or intensities, say so directly, in a calm moment: “I tend to feel this faster than you do, and that’s not a disagreement about the money — it’s a difference in how quickly the alarm fires.” Naming the mismatch as physiological rather than moral keeps it from curdling into a recurring fight where one person is cast as reckless and the other as cold, when both are simply reporting an honest reaction.

Strip the frame of reference back into view before reacting to a standalone number. Whether the trigger is a live chart or a plain paper statement, the jolt feeds on a number arriving in isolation, with no comparison point attached. Before reacting, deliberately locate the comparison that context provides — what did this account look like a year ago, two years ago, at the start of your plan — and put the current figure next to it on purpose. This doesn't require sophisticated analysis, just the discipline of refusing to let a single, isolated figure stand in for the whole picture, which is exactly the form the jolt prefers to arrive in.

The color arrives before the number does, and the feeling arrives before the thought does — so the only reliable defense is a rule made in advance that doesn't require you to think clearly in the exact moment you're least able to.

Chapter 3 — The Herd You Can't See

Why Watching Other People Run Makes You Run Faster Than the Danger Warrants

She finds out everyone else is worried before she's worried herself. It starts as a notification on her phone — a message from a group chat, three people already deep into a conversation about whether they should be "getting out" — and she reads it standing in her kitchen, coffee not yet finished, portfolio not yet checked that morning. The messages keep arriving while she reads: someone else confirming they already sold half their position, someone else asking if anyone's heard anything specific or if it's "just a feeling," someone else posting a screenshot of a headline with three exclamation points and no further comment. She hasn't looked at her own account yet. She doesn't need to, not really, to feel the specific tightening that's already started in her chest — because the danger, as far as her nervous system is concerned, isn't really located in a number she hasn't seen. It's located in the visible fact that people she trusts are already afraid, already moving, already treating this as something worth fleeing. By the time she finally opens her own account ten minutes later, she's not evaluating the number with fresh eyes. She's looking for confirmation of a fear that arrived secondhand, fully formed, before she'd generated any independent read of her own situation at all.

This is the chapter's real subject: not what triggers your own alarm directly, but what happens when you watch, or hear about, other people's alarms going off — and how powerfully that secondhand signal can override even a calm, well-reasoned independent assessment you might otherwise have made on your own.

There's a version of this that shows up even without a crowd at all, worth naming because it reveals how little the mechanism actually requires. A young professional, checking his account during a lunch break, notices nothing alarming in his own numbers — a slightly down day, nothing more. But scrolling past a financial news app afterward, he sees a auto-generated "most active" list dominated by red, sees a few unrelated posts expressing worry, sees a comment thread full of people describing their own fear in vivid, specific language. None of these people know him. None of them are reacting to anything about his actual portfolio. But the cumulative visible weight of strangers being afraid, encountered in the space of ninety seconds of scrolling, produces a felt sense of consensus — *everyone agrees this is bad* — powerful enough that he closes the app and, within the hour, sells a position that, an hour earlier, hadn't concerned him at all. The crowd, in this case, isn't people he knows. It's an anonymous accumulation of visible fear, and it works on the same ancient mechanism regardless of whether a single face in it is familiar.

A different scene: a man who owns a small retail business, watching, over the course of a single week, three other shop owners on his block quietly begin discounting inventory, one after another, each one telling him some version of the same thing — that they've heard from a supplier, or a customer, or a cousin in a related industry, that a downturn is coming, that it's smarter to move product now while people are still buying than to be caught holding it later. He hasn't seen a downturn in his own numbers. His own sales, checked honestly, are flat, not falling. But he watches his neighbors start discounting, watches the visible signal of their fear spread down the block one storefront at a time, and within a week he's discounting too — not because his own data changed, but because everyone around him started acting like the ground was shifting, and standing still while your neighbors run starts to feel like its own kind of danger, regardless of what your own numbers actually say. He cuts prices, takes a real loss on margin, and only weeks later, once the wave has passed and demand turns out to have been steady the whole time, does he recognize that he never actually checked his own situation before reacting to everyone else's.

A third scene shows the cascade traveling through the most trusted channel of all: family. A woman in her fifties receives a call from her older brother, someone she has looked to for financial guidance since they were both young, who tells her, with total conviction, that he's moved his own retirement funds into something more conservative and thinks she should seriously consider doing the same "before it's too late." She hasn't looked at her own account that day. She doesn't ask him what specifically prompted his own decision, or whether his situation — closer to retirement, differently allocated, carrying different obligations — actually resembles hers in any way that would make his move relevant to her at all. She simply absorbs his certainty as if it were information about her own portfolio, and within the day has made a parallel move, not because she independently evaluated her position, but because the person whose judgment she has trusted her whole life sounded certain, and certainty delivered by someone you love travels faster and lands harder than certainty from any stranger ever could.

A second scene shows the same mechanism operating inside a much more formal, supposedly deliberate setting, useful because it proves the cascade doesn't require an emotional group chat to take hold — a spreadsheet and a conference room will do just fine. A small nonprofit's three-person investment committee meets for what was scheduled as a routine quarterly review, during a period when the broader market has had a rough few weeks. One committee member, arriving a few minutes early, mentions to the other two, almost in passing, that she's "been hearing a lot of people talk about pulling back right now." Nobody at the table has done any independent analysis of the nonprofit's own specific investment horizon, its own specific need for the funds, or any data point beyond that one offhand remark. But the remark changes the temperature of the entire meeting before it's officially begun. Each member, not wanting to be the one voice arguing for staying the course against a room that suddenly feels uneasy, ends up voting to move a meaningful share of the endowment into cash — a decision that gets written up afterward, in the minutes, as "a prudent, considered response to market conditions," with no reference anywhere in the official record to the offhand comment that actually set the whole vote in motion. The formality of the setting didn't protect the group from the cascade. It just gave the cascade a more official-sounding vocabulary to hide inside.

What's actually happening

The economist and Nobel laureate Robert Shiller, whose research focused extensively on speculative bubbles and market psychology, wrote at length about the mechanism at work in both of these scenes: informational cascades. A cascade begins when people, faced with uncertainty, start relying not on their own private information or judgment but on the visible actions of others around them — reasoning, often correctly in isolated cases but disastrously in aggregate, that other people's decisions must reflect information they don't personally have. If enough people start selling, the thinking goes, they probably know something. This can happen even when no one in the chain actually possesses new information at all — each person is simply reacting to the person before them, and the appearance of collective knowledge builds entirely out of people copying each other's fear, with no actual signal underneath it except the growing size of the crowd itself. Shiller's broader work on "irrational exuberance" documented how these cascades run in both directions — building bubbles on the way up, and building panics on the way down — and how strongly ordinary, otherwise careful people get swept into them, because the visible behavior of a crowd is an extraordinarily persuasive signal, even when it's built on nothing more solid than everyone reacting to everyone else.

There's a deeper evolutionary layer underneath the economic mechanism, and it helps explain why the pull is so hard to resist even when you intellectually know better. Humans evolved as a profoundly social species, in small groups where the collective behavior of the group was, for most of that evolutionary history, one of the single most reliable sources of survival-relevant information available. If everyone around you suddenly ran, the correct response, across almost the entire span of human evolutionary history, was to run first and ask questions later — because the cost of being the one person who stood still while a genuine threat approached was, again and again, catastrophic, while the cost of running unnecessarily alongside everyone else was mild: some wasted energy, a little embarrassment, nothing more. This asymmetry built a strong, largely automatic tendency to treat a fleeing crowd as credible evidence of danger, independent of any specific reason to believe the danger is real. In a financial context, this same tendency gets activated by a group chat, a headline someone else reacted to first, a friend's panicked phone call — none of which constitute actual evidence about the health of your specific investments, but all of which read, to the same ancient threat-detection system, as functionally identical to watching your whole village start running.

The woman in the kitchen never independently evaluated her own account before the fear arrived. The fear arrived first, delivered by people she trusts, and her subsequent look at her own numbers was already filtered through a threat that had been pre-installed by the group. This is worth naming precisely, because it explains why "just do your own research" is such incomplete advice in these moments — by the time most people do their own research, the emotional verdict has often already been rendered by the crowd's visible behavior, and the research that follows tends to search for confirmation of that verdict rather than functioning as a genuinely independent check.

There's a related, well-documented finding worth naming here, because it explains why the pull is so strong even among people who consider themselves independent thinkers, unlikely to be swayed by a crowd. Foundational research on social conformity, including the classic line-judgment experiments conducted by psychologist Solomon Asch, found that people will frequently override their own clear, correct, independently-formed perception of a simple fact when enough other people around them appear to believe something different

— not necessarily because they're persuaded the group is right, but because the discomfort of visibly disagreeing with a unanimous group becomes its own pressure, powerful enough to bend a judgment that, alone, the person would have made confidently and correctly. Financial cascades add a second layer on top of this baseline conformity pressure: in Asch's experiments, the stakes of being wrong were social, a moment of mild embarrassment. In a market panic, the group's visible fear carries an implied stake that feels existential — not "you'll look foolish disagreeing with the room" but "everyone else may be about to avoid a catastrophe you're about to walk into" — which raises the pressure to conform substantially higher than anything a simple line-judgment task could produce, and helps explain why otherwise level-headed people abandon carefully built plans within minutes of watching a crowd start to move.

It's worth noting, too, that a cascade doesn't require a large crowd to feel overwhelming. A handful of visibly worried voices — three people in a group chat, one respected colleague, a single relative who "always seems to know what's coming" — can produce nearly the same pull as a much larger, more anonymous crowd, because the mechanism doesn't scale strictly with numbers. It scales with how much the observed behavior feels like it's coming from people whose judgment you'd normally trust, which is precisely why the fear inside a small, close group chat can spread faster and land harder than the same fear delivered by an anonymous headline with no face attached to it at all.

It's worth adding a final, practical distinction here between the two kinds of cascades this chapter has described — the anonymous, scrolling kind and the small, trusted-circle kind — because they call for slightly different vigilance. An anonymous cascade is often easier to recognize for what it is, precisely because the people in it are strangers; there's little cost to treating their fear with some skepticism. A trusted-circle cascade is harder, because dismissing it can feel like dismissing the person, not just the panic they're carrying, and that social cost is exactly what makes this second kind of cascade so much more persuasive despite being no more evidentially reliable than the first. Recognizing which kind of cascade you're inside is itself a useful first step, because the trusted-circle version requires a gentler, more relationship-aware version of the same underlying override: separating what you know from what you've heard, without it needing to feel like a rejection of the person doing the telling.

The brother-and-sister scene reveals a specific amplifier worth naming on its own: trust itself is what makes the cascade travel faster, not slower. It's tempting to assume that hearing alarming information from someone you deeply trust would prompt more scrutiny, not less — surely you'd want to check a loved one's claim as carefully as a stranger's, if not more so. The research on informational cascades suggests the opposite tends to happen in practice. The more you trust the source, the less independent verification your own judgment demands before accepting their conclusion as reliable, because trust functions, in this specific context, as a kind of pre-approved shortcut around the verification step you'd normally apply to a stranger's claim. This is a rational strategy in ordinary life — trusting people who've earned trust is, most of the time, a reasonable way to save effort. It becomes a liability specifically in moments where the trusted person is themselves reacting to fear rather than to verified information, because their fear now travels under the cover of their credibility, arriving at your doorstep pre-certified as reliable when it may be nothing more than their own unexamined jolt, one relationship removed.

There's a further layer worth adding from research on group decision-making conducted by psychologist Irving Janis, whose studies of high-stakes committee and government decisions identified a pattern he called groupthink — the tendency of cohesive groups, especially ones under time pressure or perceived threat, to suppress dissenting views and converge prematurely on a shared course of action, often without any member individually believing the group's conclusion is well-supported. Janis found that groupthink is particularly likely when a group values harmony and consensus, when there's no established practice of deliberately seeking out a devil's-advocate view, and when the group feels itself to be under outside pressure — all three conditions present, almost perfectly, in the nonprofit committee's rushed, uneasy meeting. What makes Janis's research especially useful here is his finding that groupthink doesn't require genuine agreement to produce a unanimous-looking decision. It only requires each individual member's unwillingness to be the lone dissenting voice, which means a room can arrive at a confident, unanimous-seeming verdict that not one person in it, examined privately and separately, would have reached on their own. The endowment committee's minutes describe a "considered response." What actually happened was three individually uncertain people, each one reluctant to be the holdout, converging on a decision built entirely out of that mutual reluctance.

What it costs you

The financial cost compounds specifically because cascades, by their nature, tend to peak in intensity right as the underlying situation is often closest to a turning point — the moment when fear has spread furthest and fastest is frequently the moment furthest from any actual new information, and closest to the point where the panic itself, rather than the original trigger, has become the primary story. Selling into the peak of a cascade means selling into the moment when prices have often already absorbed the worst of the news and then some, driven down further by fear feeding on fear rather than by any fresh deterioration in the underlying situation. The shop owner who discounted alongside his neighbors gave away real margin chasing a downturn that, in his own specific business, never actually arrived — he paid a real cost to synchronize with a crowd's fear rather than his own data.

The subtler cost is what this does to your confidence in your own judgment going forward. Once you've followed a crowd into a decision that turns out, in hindsight, to have been driven by nothing more than everyone reacting to everyone else, it becomes harder to trust your own read the next time — and harder, specifically, to distinguish "the crowd is reacting to real information I don't have" from "the crowd is reacting to itself." That uncertainty doesn't resolve cleanly. It tends to leave people more susceptible to the next cascade, not less, because they've learned to doubt their own independent judgment rather than learning to better distinguish signal from social noise.

There is also a specific, often-overlooked cost to being the person who started, or amplified, a cascade for others — a cost that isn't financial at all but relational. The three people in the group chat who posted first, the neighbor who discounted first and told the others a downturn was coming, become, whether they intended it or not, the source of someone else's panic-driven decision. This doesn't require malice or even confidence in the underlying claim — often the first mover in a cascade is simply the most anxious person in the group, not the best informed — but the effect on everyone downstream is the same regardless of intent, and it's worth carrying that awareness the next time you're the one reaching for the phone to warn someone else about what you're feeling, rather than what you actually know.

There's a final, structural cost worth naming that applies specifically to cascades that happen inside formal groups like the nonprofit's investment committee: once a group has made a fear-driven decision and recorded it, in writing, as a "prudent, considered response," that written record becomes its own kind of evidence the next time a similar situation arises — cited, referenced, treated as precedent, by people who weren't in the room for the original offhand comment that actually started it. The minutes don't preserve the mechanism. They preserve the outcome, stripped of the context that would let a future committee recognize the same pattern forming again. This is how institutional cascades become self-perpetuating in a way individual ones don't: the individual eventually has direct memory of what actually happened, however much that memory gets smoothed over, but the institution only has the sanitized record, which actively teaches the wrong lesson to everyone who reads it afterward.

There's a final, compounding cost specific to cascades that travel through trusted relationships rather than anonymous crowds: the damage doesn't stay contained to the financial decision itself. When the sister later realizes her brother's certainty was itself untested, something quieter than money gets strained — a small, specific erosion in how automatically she extends trust to his judgment going forward, even in domains that have nothing to do with investing. Cascades that move through families and close friendships carry this extra, non-financial tax: every panic passed along and later regretted makes the next piece of advice from that same trusted source land with slightly less unquestioned authority than it once did, whether or not that's a fair outcome for the person who was, in their own way, just as frightened as everyone downstream of them.

The overrides

Separate what you know from what you've heard, explicitly, before reacting to either. When a fear arrives secondhand — a message, a call, a headline someone else reacted to first — write down, literally, two short lists: what you have personally verified about your own specific situation, and what you've only heard secondhand about the general situation. This sounds almost mechanical, but it does real work, because cascades depend on the two categories blurring together into one undifferentiated feeling of alarm. Keeping them visibly separate breaks that blur.

The Move: delay checking your own accounts until you've had at least one hour of distance from the secondhand alarm. When a fear arrives through a group chat, a call, a headline someone else is already reacting to, resist the pull to immediately check your own position while that secondhand alarm is still fresh. Give it real time — an hour, ideally longer — before you look at your own numbers, so that when you do look, you're evaluating your actual situation rather than searching for confirmation of a fear the crowd installed in you minutes earlier. This single delay is often enough to let the initial cascade-driven spike of urgency pass, revealing whether there's still a real reason to be concerned once the secondhand panic has faded.

Count how many people in the chain have actually verified anything firsthand. When a fear is spreading through a group, ask directly, of the specific chain you're part of: how many of these people, going back to the original source, actually checked something themselves, versus simply repeating what the person before them said with added urgency? Cascades very often trace back to a single original claim, sometimes itself uncertain or partial, that has been relayed and amplified by several people who each added their own conviction without adding any new verification. Tracing the chain back even briefly frequently reveals there was only ever one actual data point underneath a great deal of borrowed certainty.

Ask, specifically, whether the crowd has new information or is just reacting to itself. Before treating a crowd's fear as evidence, ask directly: is there a specific, checkable fact behind this, or is everyone simply reacting to everyone else's reaction? This is often answerable with a few minutes of genuine checking, and the answer, more often than the moment suggests, turns out to be the latter — a cascade with no independent signal underneath it, just fear reflecting off itself.

Choose your information sources for calm, not just speed. If a specific group chat, feed, or person reliably delivers alarm before it delivers verified information, that's worth noticing as a pattern, not a one-time event. You don't need to cut people off. You do need to recognize which channels tend to arrive with the crowd's fear already attached, and weight what comes from them accordingly, rather than treating every source as equally reliable evidence about your own situation.

Find one dissenting voice before you act on a unanimous-feeling crowd. Asch's research found that conformity pressure dropped sharply the moment even a single other person in the group visibly disagreed with the majority —

the presence of just one dissenter was often enough to restore an individual's confidence in their own independent judgment. You can build the same effect deliberately: before acting on a cascade of shared fear, deliberately seek out one source, one calmer voice, one piece of contrary information, even if you have to go looking for it. You don't need it to be right. You need it to break the felt unanimity that's doing most of the persuasive work.

Ask what specifically qualifies the trusted source's situation as similar to yours, before treating their move as guidance for your own. When alarming advice arrives from someone you trust, resist the pull to accept their conclusion wholesale, and instead ask a narrow, specific question: does their timeline, their allocation, their obligations actually resemble mine closely enough for their decision to be relevant to mine at all? A sibling closer to retirement, a friend with a different risk tolerance, a colleague holding a completely different mix of assets may have made a decision that's entirely reasonable for their own situation and entirely irrelevant to yours — and trust in the person is not the same thing as relevance of the advice.

In any group decision, assign someone the explicit job of disagreeing before the discussion starts. Janis's research on groupthink found that formally designating a devil's-advocate role — someone whose job, agreed on in advance, is to argue the other side regardless of their personal view — measurably reduces premature convergence, because it gives dissent a sanctioned, expected place in the conversation rather than requiring any one person to spontaneously risk being the lone holdout. If you sit on any committee, board, or household decision involving shared money, build this role in before the meeting starts, not after the uneasy mood has already taken hold.

A crowd running is powerful evidence that a crowd is afraid. It is not evidence that you, specifically, are in danger — check which one you're actually reacting to before you move.

Chapter 4 — The Story That Arrives Just in Time

Why the Reason You Sold Almost Never Came First

He can tell you exactly why he sold, in clean, confident sentences, with no hesitation at all. Rising rates, a specific concern about the sector, a general sense that valuations had gotten ahead of themselves, a nagging feeling he'd had "for a while" that this was coming. It's a good story. It's coherent, it references real, legitimate concerns that plenty of careful, sober analysts were also discussing at the time, and it makes him sound, telling it to a friend over dinner weeks later, like someone who read the situation correctly and acted on sound judgment. There's only one problem with the story, which he doesn't mention, possibly because he's genuinely stopped noticing it himself: the decision to sell happened in about ninety seconds, sitting on his couch, phone in hand, after seeing a single alarming headline scroll past — and the rates, the sector concern, the valuation worry, the nagging feeling "for a while," all of that got assembled afterward, over the following hour, as he searched for reasons that would explain a decision his body had already made before any of those reasons had been consciously considered. He's not lying when he tells the story. He genuinely believes it. That's what makes this mechanism so difficult to catch — the story doesn't feel invented. It feels like memory.

Picture a different version of the same shape, in a completely different setting. A retired teacher, watching her modest but carefully built portfolio drop meaningfully over the course of a difficult week, calls her adult daughter and explains, at real length and with genuine conviction, that she's decided to move everything into something safer because "the whole system feels unstable right now, and I've thought about this for a long time." Her daughter, who has talked to her mother regularly throughout this period, gently points out that this doesn't match what her mother said just five days earlier, when she'd described feeling calm and committed to her plan. The mother doesn't remember it that way. She's not being dishonest — she has genuinely reconstructed her own recent history to match her current feeling, smoothing over the actual sequence of events until the story reads as a long-considered decision rather than what it actually was: a fast, fear-driven reaction from three days ago that her mind has spent the time since dressing up in the language of deliberation.

A third version, briefer but worth including because it shows the mechanism operating even in a decision that never actually gets executed: a young couple, mid-argument about whether to pause contributions to a joint investment account after a rough month, watch one partner build, in real time, an increasingly confident case for pausing — citing a cousin's advice, a podcast episode, a vague sense that "everyone's saying to be careful right now." The other partner, who was in the room fifteen minutes earlier when the whole conversation started with a single sentence — "I just saw the balance and got scared" — points this out gently. The first partner pauses, genuinely surprised, and admits, after a moment, that the fear really did come first, and the reasons arrived afterward while searching for a way to make the fear sound sensible out loud. The couple ultimately doesn't pause the contributions. But the moment is instructive precisely because it was caught early, mid-construction, before the story had time to fully harden into a settled, confidently-recalled account of events.

A fourth scene shows the story arriving not to explain a sale, but to explain a much smaller, easier-to-overlook decision: a man who has stopped opening his investment app for three weeks straight, after a rough stretch, explains to a friend, when asked, that he's "just not really focused on that right now, there's a lot going on at work." The explanation is plausible. It's also, if he's honest with himself, not the actual sequence — the actual sequence is that he checked once, three weeks ago, felt a sharp, unpleasant jolt, and has been quietly avoiding the app ever since, a decision his mind has since relabeled as busyness rather than avoidance, because "busy" is a far more comfortable story than "afraid to look." No sale occurred here. But the same story-building machinery ran anyway, on a decision to not act, proving that the mechanism isn't limited to explaining dramatic moves — it works just as readily on quiet withdrawals that never show up as a single traceable transaction.

A fourth scene, briefer, is worth adding because it shows the story-building mechanism attaching itself not to a sale but to a decision to stay uninsured against a risk. A homeowner, having let a supplemental policy lapse two years earlier during a stretch when money was tight, watches a neighbor's property suffer real damage from an event the lapsed policy would have covered. Within days, he's telling anyone who asks a fluent, confident account of why he let the policy go — the premiums had gotten disproportionate, the coverage overlapped with something else he already had, he'd "run the numbers" and decided it wasn't worth it. Some of this is even true in fragments. What's missing from the account, entirely, is the actual reason, which his spouse remembers clearly and which he no longer does: the policy lapsed because a renewal notice arrived during a chaotic week and got set aside, unopened, and by the time anyone noticed, the grace period had passed. There was no considered analysis. There was an accident of timing, followed, months later, by a fully-formed justification that arrived only once the absence of coverage became something worth explaining. The story didn't get built to justify a panic-driven sale this time. It got built to justify an ordinary, forgettable oversight — proof that the same rationalization machinery runs on far smaller inputs than a ninety-second panic, whenever the gap between "what actually happened" and "what I'd like to have been true" needs closing.

What's actually happening

This is one of the most well-established findings in the study of judgment and decision-making, and it comes directly from the foundational work of Daniel Kahneman and Amos Tversky, whose research on heuristics and biases reshaped how psychology and economics understand human choice. Kahneman, in his later work synthesizing decades of this research, described the mind as operating through two broad systems: a fast, automatic, largely unconscious system generating quick impressions and reactions, and a slower, more effortful system capable of deliberate reasoning and careful analysis. The critical, uncomfortable finding is this: the slow system doesn't typically originate decisions from a neutral starting point. Far more often, it functions as a justification engine for conclusions the fast system has already reached — constructing plausible, coherent, genuinely convincing reasons for a choice that was actually made well before the reasoning began. This isn't occasional dishonesty. It's the normal, default operation of how these two systems interact, and it happens so smoothly that the person doing it has no subjective sense that anything has been reordered.

There's a further finding from Kahneman and Tversky's broader body of work worth naming here, because it explains why the justification engine is so rarely caught in the act: it doesn't generate weak, obviously flimsy reasons. It generates good ones — real, legitimate, defensible considerations that a careful analyst might independently raise on their own merits. The rates were rising. The sector concerns were real, and other people were discussing them. This is precisely what makes post-hoc rationalization so much harder to catch than an outright lie: a lie can be checked against the facts and found false. A rationalization is often built entirely out of true facts, selected and assembled after the decision rather than before it, which means the content itself passes every honesty check you could apply to it. What fails the check isn't the facts. It's the sequence — and sequence is exactly the piece of information an after-the-fact story is least equipped to preserve accurately.

Psychologists studying this broader pattern sometimes describe it as motivated reasoning or post-hoc rationalization — the mind working backward from a conclusion to construct supporting evidence, rather than working forward from evidence to a conclusion, all while the person doing it experiences the process as if it ran in the correct, forward direction. This is not a rare failure mode reserved for careless thinkers. Research in this area has repeatedly found the pattern present even in highly intelligent, highly analytical people — arguably more so in some cases, because a sharper mind is simply more capable of constructing a genuinely persuasive story after the fact, persuasive enough to convince not just other people but the person telling it.

Here's why this matters so much for the specific pattern of panic-selling: the story that arrives after a panic-driven sale doesn't feel like a rationalization from the inside. It feels like the actual reason, recalled accurately. This is what makes panic selling so difficult for people to recognize in themselves, even in hindsight, even when they're specifically looking for it. The man on the couch isn't in denial about having panicked. He genuinely doesn't experience it that way anymore, because his mind has since done the normal, automatic work of building a forward-facing narrative — rates, sector concerns, valuation, a feeling "for a while" — that reads, to him, as the actual sequence of events. Ask him directly whether he panicked, and he'll say no, with complete sincerity, because the story he's now carrying genuinely doesn't include a panic. The panic got edited out somewhere in the retelling, replaced by something that sounds like foresight.

There's a specific reason the mind does this work so eagerly, rather than simply leaving the decision unexplained. Humans have a strong, well-documented drive toward what psychologists call cognitive consistency — a discomfort with holding two conflicting self-images at once, such as "I am a careful, rational investor" and "I just made an impulsive, fear-driven decision in ninety seconds." When those two images collide, the mind tends to resolve the tension not by accepting the uncomfortable one, but by quietly revising the story until the tension disappears — in this case, by upgrading "impulsive reaction" into "considered decision," a much more comfortable story to carry, and one that requires no uncomfortable update to the underlying self-image at all. This drive toward consistency is closely related to what the psychologist Leon Festinger, in his foundational research on the topic, called cognitive dissonance

— the genuinely uncomfortable mental state produced by holding two contradictory beliefs at once, and the powerful, largely automatic motivation to resolve that discomfort, often by revising the less flattering belief rather than confronting it directly. Festinger's research found that people will go to considerable lengths, including rewriting their own memory of events, to avoid sitting inside that contradiction — which is precisely the work being done, quietly and invisibly, in the hour after a panic-driven sale.

It's worth being specific about what the retired teacher's daughter actually witnessed, because it illustrates how fast this rewriting can happen and how convincing it becomes even to the person who lived through the real sequence. Five days separated her mother's calm, plan-committed conversation from her fear-driven, plan-abandoning one. In a healthy, accurate memory, that shift would register as exactly what it was: a sudden change, triggered by something specific, worth examining. Instead, by the time of the second phone call, the intervening five days had already been smoothed over into a single, continuous narrative — "I've been thinking about this for a long time" — that erased the actual discontinuity entirely. This isn't a memory failure in the sense of forgetting facts. The mother still remembered the calm conversation perfectly well if asked about it directly. What had changed was the story connecting the two moments, rewritten to feel like a gradual, considered evolution rather than what it actually was: a sharp break, triggered by a specific, nameable event, five days prior.

A related, deeply relevant body of research comes from psychologists Richard Nisbett and Timothy Wilson, whose studies of introspection found something genuinely unsettling about how little direct access people have to their own actual mental processes, even while feeling completely confident they do. In a range of experiments, Nisbett and Wilson found that people routinely, confidently reported reasons for their choices and judgments that demonstrably were not the actual causes of those choices — the real causal factors were often ones the participants had no conscious access to at all, while the reasons they offered, sincerely and fluently, were constructed after the fact to fit the choice already made. Their research described this as a case of people acting as "naive scientists," building plausible causal theories about their own behavior using the same general-knowledge reasoning they'd use to explain someone else's behavior, rather than through any privileged inside access to what had actually happened in their own minds. This is worth sitting with because it removes a comforting assumption most people carry without examining it: that whatever you say about *why* you made a decision must be true, since presumably nobody has better access to your own mind than you do. Nisbett and Wilson's research says otherwise. The felt sense of introspective certainty — "I know why I did that" — is not reliable evidence that you actually do, and the confidence with which the reason arrives tells you nothing about its accuracy. The man on the couch isn't unusual in this. He's doing exactly what the research predicts any of us would do, sincerely and fluently, without ever noticing the gap.

What it costs you

The most direct cost is that a story built to protect your self-image, rather than to accurately describe what happened, cannot teach you anything useful about how to behave differently next time. If the man on the couch genuinely believes he sold because of carefully weighed macroeconomic reasoning, he has no reason to build any defenses against the next ninety-second, headline-triggered impulse — as far as his own memory is concerned, that impulse never happened. The retired teacher, believing she made a long-considered decision, has no reason to examine what actually happened in the five days before her call to her daughter, which means the same five-day pattern is fully available to repeat itself the next time a difficult week arrives.

There's a compounding cost specific to investing: this same story-building mechanism doesn't stop working after the sale. It continues afterward, shaping how the outcome itself gets remembered. If the sale turns out badly — prices recover, and the sale locked in a loss that a few more weeks of patience would have avoided — the same mind that built the original story will often build a second one to explain the bad outcome without revisiting the original decision honestly: "I couldn't have known it would recover so fast," or "the situation was genuinely different this time," each of which may contain a grain of truth while still functioning primarily to protect the story that the original decision was sound. This means the single most valuable kind of feedback available to you — an honest look at what a panic-driven decision actually cost — gets quietly filtered out before it can do any good, chapter after chapter, decision after decision, unless something interrupts the pattern deliberately.

There's a final, relational cost worth naming, because both scenes in this chapter involve another person hearing the polished story. The friend across the dinner table, the daughter on the phone, absorb a version of events that isn't accurate, and they calibrate their own trust and their own future advice around a story that was never quite true. If the man's friend later finds himself in a similar situation, he may reasonably lean on his memory of his friend's "considered, well-reasoned" call as a model worth following, not realizing he's actually about to imitate a ninety-second panic dressed up as analysis. This is how a single unexamined panic can quietly propagate well beyond the person who experienced it — not through any deliberate deception, but through the ordinary, well-meaning act of sharing a story that both teller and listener sincerely believe to be accurate. The rewritten story doesn't need malice to do damage. It only needs to sound coherent enough to be worth repeating. The rewritten story doesn't just mislead the person who tells it. It quietly misinforms everyone who hears it and takes it as a genuine account of good decision-making under pressure.

There's a fourth cost, subtler than the rest, that shows up over the span of years rather than any single decision: the steady accumulation of a personal financial history that reads, in the telling, as far more consistent and deliberate than it actually was. A person who has quietly rewritten five or six panic-driven decisions over a decade, each time smoothing the sequence into something that sounds like foresight, eventually arrives at a self-narrative — "I've always made careful, considered calls with my money" — that has almost no relationship to what their actual account statements would show. This isn't harmless self-flattery. It actively degrades the one piece of self-knowledge most useful for preventing the next panic: an accurate sense of exactly how vulnerable you actually are to this specific pattern, which the smoothed story has spent years quietly erasing the evidence for.

The overrides

Write the reason down before you act, not after. This is the single most direct countermeasure to post-hoc rationalization, because it removes the opportunity for the story to be built retroactively. Before selling anything in response to a sudden concern, write, in a few sentences, the actual reason, right now, with a timestamp. Not the polished version — the raw one. If the honest sentence is closer to "I saw a scary headline and felt like I had to do something," write that. This written record becomes a check against the smoother story your mind will otherwise construct over the following hours, and it's often the only reliable evidence, later, of what actually happened first.

The Move: build a mandatory "reasons list" you fill out before any panic-adjacent sale is allowed to execute. Create a short, standing list of questions you must answer, in writing, before selling in response to sudden fear: What specific new information changed today? Did I have this concern a week ago, in writing, before today's trigger? Would I make this same decision if I couldn't see the price move that triggered it? Answering these honestly, in the moment, before acting, makes it far harder for a ninety-second impulse to disguise itself as a long-considered decision — because the disguise has to be built in writing, right now, under your own scrutiny, rather than assembled comfortably over the following days.

Revisit your own written reasons afterward, specifically to check for drift. A week or two after any significant financial decision made under stress, go back and reread what you wrote at the time, and compare it honestly to the story you're currently telling yourself and others about why you did it. If the story has grown more confident, more coherent, more "I'd been thinking about this for a while" than what you actually wrote in the moment, that drift is worth noticing directly — not as self-criticism, but as useful data about how your own mind processes decisions made under threat.

Tell someone the raw version, not just the polished one. Choose one person you trust enough to hear the unflattering truth, and practice telling them the actual sequence — "I saw the headline, I felt panicked, I sold" — rather than only the version with the reasons attached. Saying the raw sequence out loud, to another person, makes it much harder for your own memory to quietly overwrite it later, because you've now created an external witness to what actually happened first.

Look for the specific signature of a rewritten story: too much coherence, too fast. A genuinely considered decision, reflected on honestly, usually comes with some acknowledged uncertainty, some remembered back-and-forth, some "I went back and forth on this for a while." A story that arrives fully formed, entirely confident, with no rough edges and no memory of doubt, is worth treating as a flag rather than a comfort — real deliberation tends to leave some visible mess behind it, and an unusually clean narrative is often a sign that the mess has been edited out rather than that it never existed.

Treat your own stated reasons as a hypothesis, not a fact, until you've checked them against a timestamp. Fluent, confident recall is not the same thing as accurate recall — the two feel identical from the inside but are not reliably connected, which is the entire reason a rewritten story can feel so convincing to the person telling it. Build the habit of treating any confident, fluent explanation you offer for a financial decision — especially one made under stress — as a claim worth checking rather than a report worth trusting automatically. The check is simple: does a contemporaneous record (a written note, a message to someone else, a calendar entry) actually support the story, or does the story only exist in memory, reconstructed after the fact? A reason with no paper trail predating the decision deserves real skepticism, regardless of how convinced you feel while telling it.

Apply the same scrutiny to decisions you didn't make, not only the ones you did. The rewriting mechanism works just as smoothly on avoidance as it does on action — "I've just been busy" standing in for "I've been afraid to look" is the same process wearing a quieter disguise. Periodically ask, of any financial task you've been putting off: is there a genuinely practical reason this hasn't happened, or is there a jolt sitting underneath the delay that a more comfortable story has already covered over?

The reasons you give for a panic-driven decision are almost never the reasons that came first — write down what's actually happening before your mind gets a chance to improve the story.

Chapter 5 — The Wrong Kind of Fast

Why the Speed That Saves You From a Swerving Car Wrecks You in a Downturn

A truck drifts into her lane, and she's already turned the wheel before the thought "that truck is drifting into my lane" has fully formed in words. There was no deliberation. There was no weighing of options. There was a threat, a body already moving in response to it, and a correction executed with a speed that no careful, step-by-step analysis could have matched — analysis that, in that half-second, would have gotten her killed. This is fast thinking working exactly as intended: a genuine emergency, a genuinely correct response, executed at a speed only an automatic system can achieve. Nobody would tell her, afterward, that she should have thought it through more carefully. The speed was the entire point, and it saved her.

Three weeks later, sitting at her kitchen table, she watches her investment account drop by an amount that, converted to a percentage, looks alarmingly similar to how close that truck had gotten. Her body responds with the same fast, automatic system that turned the wheel — full alertness, narrowed focus, an urgent pull toward immediate action — and she sells a meaningful chunk of a long-term position within minutes of the drop registering, with the same decisive speed that saved her life on the highway. Only this time, the speed doesn't save her from anything. There was no truck. There was a normal, if uncomfortable, market movement inside an account built with exactly this kind of movement anticipated, and the fast system that correctly read danger in a swerving vehicle has, in this second context, mistaken a completely different kind of situation for the same emergency — because it was never built to tell the two apart. It only knows how to detect the shape of "something bad is happening quickly," and it responds to that shape identically, regardless of whether the underlying situation actually rewards speed or punishes it.

A second scene, months later, involving no near-miss at all. A man who has run a small consulting business successfully for over a decade — someone whose entire professional reputation rests on making fast, confident calls under pressure, reading a room and deciding quickly, a skill that has genuinely served him extremely well across an entire career — applies that exact same fast-decision confidence to a sudden downturn in his retirement account. He treats the decision the way he'd treat a fast-moving negotiation: gather the visible facts quickly, trust his gut, commit, move on. It's the identical cognitive style that built his business. Applied here, in a domain where the fastest read is very often the worst one, that same confident speed leads him to lock in a significant loss within an hour of a downturn beginning — a downturn that, given the kind of broad, diversified position he held, historically resolved itself over a timeframe measured in months or years, not hours. His fast-decision instinct wasn't wrong in general. It was simply applied to a problem with a completely different time structure than the ones it had been sharpened on.

A third scene brings the same mismatch into an entirely physical, non-financial arena, useful precisely because it makes the pattern visible from the outside. A volunteer emergency responder, trained for years to make split-second calls at the scene of an accident — assess, act, move, no hesitation, because hesitation costs lives in that specific context — describes, almost sheepishly, how that exact training seems to switch on during ordinary financial stress, producing an urge to "just act" that he now recognizes doesn't belong there. He's learned to notice it precisely because his training was formal and explicit enough that he can name it when it fires in the wrong context — most people never get an equivalent, explicit label for their own fast-decision instincts, which makes it much harder for them to catch the same mismatch happening quietly inside a much less obviously "trained" reflex.

A fourth scene brings the mismatch into a domain adjacent to investing but structurally distinct from it, worth including because it shows the same wrong-kind-of-fast pattern corrupting a decision that unfolds over months rather than minutes. A woman running a small catering business, watching a major, reliable client suddenly cancel a standing contract with only a vague explanation, feels the identical fast-decision urgency the truck and the portfolio both produced — and within the same afternoon, without gathering any further information about whether the cancellation reflects a problem specific to her business or something unrelated on the client's end, she lays off two part-time staff and turns down a smaller booking she'd tentatively held space for, reasoning, in the moment, that she needs to "move fast to protect what's left." Three weeks later, the client calls back, apologetic, explaining the cancellation had nothing to do with her work at all — an internal budget freeze, unrelated to her, now lifted. The staff she let go have taken other work. The booking she turned down went to a competitor. Nothing about the original threat required an afternoon's response; the actual problem, examined honestly, had a timeline measured in weeks, plenty of room for a slower, better-informed decision. But the speed felt like competence in the moment, the same way it felt like competence to the consultant reading a room — and by the time the slower truth arrived, several fast, confident decisions had already been made and could not be un-made.

What's actually happening

Daniel Kahneman's dual-system framework, introduced in the previous chapter, has a second, equally important half worth examining directly here: not just that the fast system (System 1) often generates the conclusions the slow system (System 2) later justifies, but that System 1 is genuinely, legitimately excellent at certain categories of problem, and genuinely, predictably bad at others — and the difference between those two categories is exactly the difference between a swerving truck and a falling portfolio.

System 1 excels at problems with a specific shape: fast-moving, high-stakes, requiring an immediate physical response, where the relevant information is direct, sensory, and simple — a truck, a loud noise, a raised fist. It evolved, across an enormous span of time, precisely for problems shaped like this, and it remains extraordinarily well-tuned for them; nothing about modern life has made this category of danger obsolete, and nothing about System 1's performance here has degraded.

System 2, by contrast, is suited to a different shape of problem: slower-moving, requiring the weighing of multiple pieces of abstract, often conflicting information, where the correct answer isn't available through instinct because the situation itself is historically unprecedented for the individual facing it, or requires holding several variables in mind at once rather than reacting to one immediate signal. A market downturn is, structurally, almost always this second kind of problem — it unfolds over days, weeks, or months, not milliseconds; the "correct" response depends on abstract factors like your specific timeline, your diversification, your actual need for the money in the near term, none of which are available through instinct; and the visible, immediate signal — a falling number — is often actively misleading about the appropriate response, in a way a swerving truck never is.

The trouble is that System 1 doesn't check which category a problem belongs to before responding. It responds to the *shape* of urgency — fast, negative, demanding attention — and a market downturn, viewed on a screen updating in real time, produces exactly that shape, even though the underlying problem is structurally nothing like a swerving truck. Kahneman himself, in describing the broader implications of this research, was careful to note that System 1 isn't unreliable or defective — it's simply being asked, constantly, in modern financial contexts, to solve a category of problem it was never built for, using tools honed for a completely different category, and it does so with exactly the same confidence it brings to problems it's genuinely well-suited for. That confidence is precisely the danger. System 1 doesn't announce "I am not well-suited to this problem." It just delivers a fast, decisive read, indistinguishable, from the inside, whether the underlying problem was a truck or a ten-year retirement plan.

The consultant's story adds a further wrinkle worth naming plainly: expertise in one domain of fast decision-making does not transfer to another. His years of successful, fast, confident calls in business negotiations built genuine skill — but that skill was built and calibrated on a specific category of problem, with its own specific feedback loops and time structure, and it does not automatically generalize to a domain with a completely different structure, even though the *feeling* of confident, fast decision-making feels identical across both. Skilled fast-thinkers are, if anything, sometimes more vulnerable here, not less, because their fast system has been so well-rewarded in one arena that they extend its authority into a second arena without recalibrating for the fact that the two problems don't actually share a shape, only a speed.

It helps to be specific about what actually distinguishes the two categories of problem, because the distinction is learnable even though System 1 doesn't apply it automatically. A genuine System 1 problem has three features together: the window for response is measured in seconds, the correct response is largely the same regardless of which specific details you missed, and waiting to gather more information doesn't actually improve the decision because the information you'd need arrives too late to use. The swerving truck has all three — you have a second or less, the correct response (turn away from the threat) doesn't depend on knowing the other driver's reason for drifting, and there's no version of "wait and gather more data" that helps. A market downturn fails all three tests simultaneously: the window for a considered response is realistically measured in days or weeks, not seconds; the correct response depends heavily on details — your specific timeline, your specific need for the money, the specific cause of the downturn — that are not yet knowable in the first few minutes; and waiting genuinely does improve the decision, because more information becomes available the longer you wait, which is the opposite of how a true emergency behaves. Running this three-part check, even quickly, is often enough to reveal which category a given moment actually belongs to.

There's a further, complicating layer worth adding from the research of psychologist Gary Klein, whose studies of expert decision-making under real-world time pressure — firefighters, emergency-room clinicians, military commanders — developed what's known as recognition-primed decision-making: the finding that genuine experts, in genuine high-speed domains, often do make excellent fast decisions, not through slow deliberation but by rapidly recognizing a situation as matching a pattern they've encountered many times before, and acting on that recognition almost instantly. Klein's research complicates the simple "fast is always dangerous" reading of this chapter in an important way — fast decisions made by a genuine expert, inside their actual domain of expertise, are frequently very good, not despite the speed but because of the deep, well-calibrated pattern library the speed is drawing on. The catering business owner's fast read on a canceled kitchen order, or a supplier running late, might well be exactly this kind of well-calibrated expert recognition, built from years of real feedback in that specific domain. The trouble, and this is the piece that connects Klein's research back to the rest of the chapter, is that recognition-primed decision-making only works inside the specific domain where the pattern library was actually built through repeated, direct feedback — and a financial downturn, for almost everyone reading this book, is not that domain. The consultant's confidence was real expertise, misapplied. The catering owner's twenty years of reading a kitchen crisis correctly said nothing reliable about how to read a client's silence. Klein's own research is, in this sense, not a rebuttal of this chapter's warning but a sharper version of it: fast thinking is trustworthy only inside the narrow domain where it was actually trained by extensive, direct, corrective feedback — and almost nobody's fast financial instincts meet that bar, however excellent their fast instincts are somewhere else. It's worth naming, too, what genuine, well-calibrated financial expertise built through this kind of feedback loop would actually require, if only to show how rarely the conditions are met: it would need a person to make many decisions of a similar type, receive fast and unambiguous feedback on whether each one was correct, and repeat this cycle enough times to build a reliable pattern library — the same structure Klein found in firefighters who'd worked hundreds of live fires, or ER clinicians who'd triaged thousands of patients. A single investor, even a diligent one, experiences a handful of genuine market downturns across an entire lifetime, with feedback that arrives slowly, is easily confounded by other factors, and is rarely unambiguous even in hindsight. There simply isn't enough repetition, of a similar enough kind, with clean enough feedback, for ordinary experience to build the kind of fast expertise Klein documented elsewhere. This isn't a criticism of any individual investor's diligence. It's a structural fact about the problem itself, and it's exactly why the overrides in this chapter lean on borrowed structure — a written rule, a trusted second opinion — rather than on trying to accelerate your way to expertise you have no realistic path to building through direct experience alone.

What it costs you

The direct financial cost is straightforward and well worth naming plainly: decisions made at System 1 speed, applied to a System 2 problem, tend to lock in outcomes at exactly the moment the underlying situation is most extreme and least representative of where things settle once the initial shock passes. Selling within minutes of a drop means selling at close to the most negative point System 1 could detect, before any of the slower, more complete information — how the situation actually developed over the following days or weeks — had any chance to arrive and inform the decision.

The subtler cost is a kind of mismatched confidence that compounds over time. Because System 1 delivers its verdicts with total, unwavering conviction regardless of whether it's suited to the problem, people who panic-sell rarely experience the decision, in the moment, as uncertain or rushed. It feels exactly as confident as the correct, fast call to swerve away from the truck — which means the internal warning signal that might otherwise say "slow down, this doesn't feel like a problem I should be deciding quickly" never fires. The confidence itself becomes part of the trap, because a decision that feels this certain doesn't feel like something that needs to be double-checked.

There's a third cost that shows up specifically in people whose professional lives reward fast thinking, like the consultant in this chapter's second scene: a growing, unexamined blind spot around exactly the domain where their fast instincts are least reliable. Because their speed has been repeatedly rewarded elsewhere, they tend to under-invest in building the slower structures — a written plan, a standing rule, a trusted second opinion — that would otherwise catch a misapplied System 1 call, reasoning, understandably but incorrectly, that their track record of good fast decisions should generalize here too. The people most confident in their own snap judgment are frequently the people least likely to have built any external check against it, precisely because they've rarely needed one before.

There's a fourth cost worth adding, specific to households and partnerships rather than individuals: when one person in a shared financial decision operates at System 1 speed and the other operates at System 2 speed, the mismatch itself becomes a source of conflict independent of whether either read turns out to be correct. The fast-deciding partner experiences the slower one as indecisive, overly cautious, unable to act when action is needed. The slower-deciding partner experiences the fast one as reckless, unwilling to gather basic information before committing to something irreversible. Both are, in a narrow sense, describing the same underlying mismatch accurately —

they're just standing on opposite sides of it, each one convinced their own processing speed is the correct default rather than one legitimate style among several. Couples and business partners who never name this difference explicitly tend to relitigate the same argument, in a new financial costume, every time a fast-moving situation arises, without ever addressing the actual, structural mismatch underneath it.

The overrides

Name the problem's actual time structure before responding to its urgency. When a financial situation triggers an urgent, fast-decision feeling, ask directly: does this actually require a response in the next five minutes, or does it only feel like it does? A swerving truck genuinely requires a five-minute response — arguably a five-second one. A portfolio drop, in the overwhelming majority of cases, does not, regardless of how urgent it feels. Naming this distinction explicitly, out loud if needed, gives System 2 a specific, answerable question to engage with, rather than leaving the urgency to run uncontested.

The Move: install a deliberate speed mismatch — force every financial decision above a threshold you set now to take at least as long as a "slow" decision requires. Pick a dollar or percentage threshold today, while calm, above which any sell decision must go through a fixed, non-negotiable process: written reasoning, a wait period, ideally a conversation with someone else before execution. This directly counteracts System 1's advantage, because System 1's power comes entirely from speed — remove the speed, by rule, and System 2 gets the time it needs to actually engage, rather than being outrun before it starts.

Borrow expertise from a domain built for this specific time structure, not your own fastest instincts. If your own fast-decision skill was built in a different arena — business, medicine, any high-speed profession — recognize explicitly that this skill doesn't transfer to a slow-moving financial decision just because it produces the same confident feeling. Build a standing relationship with someone whose actual expertise matches the slower time structure of financial planning, and route decisions above your threshold through them, specifically to interrupt the false transfer of confidence from one domain to another.

Practice noticing the confidence itself as a signal worth questioning, not trusting. When a financial decision feels completely certain and urgent, treat that specific combination — certainty plus urgency — as a flag worth examining rather than a green light. Slow, well-reasoned financial decisions often feel less certain in the moment, not more, precisely because they're weighing genuine tradeoffs. A decision that feels perfectly obvious and needs to happen right now is worth a second look specifically because of how obvious and urgent it feels.

Ask a trusted, calmer third party the same three-part question when you can't trust your own answer to it. Sometimes the acute state you're in makes it genuinely hard to answer the emergency check honestly, even when you know the question. In those moments, having a standing arrangement with a specific person — a partner, a friend, a financial professional — whose job is simply to answer the same three questions from outside your own adrenaline, can substitute for the self-assessment you're temporarily not well positioned to make.

This isn't outsourcing the decision. It's borrowing a calmer nervous system's read on the same three facts, for exactly as long as your own is compromised.

Run the three-part emergency check before treating any financial moment as a true emergency. Ask, specifically: is my window for response really seconds, not days? Does the correct response not depend on information I don't have yet? Would waiting genuinely fail to improve this decision? If the honest answer to any of the three is no — and for financial decisions, it almost always is — you're looking at a System 2 problem wearing a System 1 costume, and the costume is the only thing making it feel urgent.

Name the speed mismatch explicitly in any shared financial decision, before it becomes a fight about something else. If you make financial decisions jointly with a partner, business co-owner, or family member, and you process urgency at noticeably different speeds, say so plainly, in a calm moment, as a description of style rather than a character judgment: "I tend to want to act fast under pressure, and you tend to want to gather more information first — neither is wrong, but we should agree in advance whose process governs decisions above a certain size." This single conversation, had once, calmly, prevents the mismatch from being relitigated as a character dispute every time a fast-moving situation actually arises.

Ask whether your fast instinct was actually built here, through real feedback, before trusting it. Borrowing Klein's framework directly: before deferring to a fast, confident financial read, ask specifically whether you've had the kind of repeated, direct, corrective feedback in this exact domain that produces genuine expert recognition — years of seeing similar situations play out and learning, concretely, which reads were right. For almost every reader, in almost every acute financial moment, the honest answer is no, which means the fast read deserves to be treated as an untrained hunch, not an expert's pattern match, however confident it feels.

Speed that saves you from a truck will wreck you in a downturn — the two problems only share a feeling, not a shape, and telling them apart is the entire job.

Chapter 6 — The Floor That Isn't There

Why Not Knowing Where the Bottom Is Frightens You More Than Knowing It's Bad

She could handle a number. What she couldn't handle was not knowing if there was a bottom to it. Watching her account fall over the course of a week, she found herself doing something strange: repeatedly opening the app not to check the current number, which she already knew was bad, but almost as if she were checking whether the falling had stopped — and each time it hadn't, each time the number was a little lower than the last check, something in her chest tightened further, not because the absolute size of the loss had grown especially large, but because the falling itself, with no visible floor, felt like it could theoretically continue forever. If someone had told her, with total certainty, on day one, "this will fall exactly this much and then stop," she suspects — and says so, later, to a friend — that she would have found the whole week far more bearable, even if the final number had been worse than what she actually experienced. It wasn't the size of the loss that broke her composure. It was the absence of a floor to stand on while it was happening.

A different version of the same fear, in a completely different setting: a man in the early stages of launching a small business, watching his personal savings — which he'd committed, in part, to funding the launch — shrink faster than his projections had anticipated, during a stretch where new client contracts were slower to materialize than planned. The actual number remaining was, by any reasonable external measure, still enough to continue for several more months. But he found himself unable to sleep, specifically because he had no reliable way to know whether the current rate of decline would continue, accelerate, or level off — the trajectory, not the current position, was the thing he couldn't get calm about. He ended up making a fast, costly decision to take on a smaller, worse-fitting client contract purely to stop the number from falling, even though it derailed the more strategic plan he'd built the business around, because the open-endedness of "I don't know when this stops" had become more unbearable than a known, worse, but bounded outcome would have been.

A third version shows how the same open-endedness can attach to a decision rather than a decline. A young couple, partway through selling a home in a slowing market, receive a lowball offer they weren't expecting and, more unsettling than the number itself, no clear signal about whether it represents where the market has settled or merely where one cautious buyer happened to land. Neither of them can find a reliable way to know whether waiting will bring a better offer or a worse one, and that specific not-knowing — not the offer itself, which they could calmly reject on its own terms — is what pushes them, within two days, toward accepting a price well below what a few more weeks of patience would likely have produced. They weren't afraid of a bad number. They were afraid of an unresolved one, and accepting the offer, however costly, ended the not-knowing immediately.

A fourth scene shows the same open-endedness attaching itself to a health-adjacent financial decision, useful because it strips away the market entirely and isolates the mechanism at its purest. A man in his thirties, recently informed by his employer that a round of layoffs is coming "sometime in the next two quarters," with no further detail available about timing, scope, or whether his own role is at risk, finds the two quarters of not-knowing considerably more disruptive to his daily functioning than the eventual layoff itself, when it comes, turns out to be. He empties a taxable investment account he'd been building for years into a low-yield cash equivalent within the first week of hearing the news — not because his actual financial need has changed yet, and not because he's calculated that he'll need the money imminently, but because doing something, anything, concrete and irreversible, felt like the only available response to a threat that had no visible edges. When the layoff eventually arrives, four months later, it turns out to affect a different department entirely. He never needed the cash. What he needed, and never got, was a way to tolerate four months of not knowing — and the account he liquidated to buy that tolerance had, in the meantime, missed a period of real growth he can't get back.

What's actually happening

The psychologist Richard Lazarus, whose research on stress and coping shaped much of how the field understands emotional response to threat, developed what's known as appraisal theory: the finding that a stressor's emotional impact depends not just on the objective severity of the threat, but heavily on how the person appraises it — including, critically, how controllable and how predictable the threat is perceived to be. Lazarus's research, and the substantial body of work that followed it, found consistently that unpredictable, open-ended threats generate more sustained stress than threats of equal or even greater objective severity that come with a known endpoint or a clear sense of scope. A known bad outcome can be appraised, planned around, and — eventually — accepted. An unknown, ongoing, open-ended one cannot be fully appraised at all, because the appraisal process requires information the situation simply isn't providing, and the mind, denied that information, tends to fill the gap with worst-case simulation rather than settling into calm uncertainty.

This connects directly to a related and well-documented finding sometimes called intolerance of uncertainty — a well-studied vulnerability factor in anxiety research showing that many people find genuine not-knowing considerably more distressing than a bad-but-known outcome, even when the not-knowing is objectively less severe on average. Applied to the falling account: the woman checking the app repeatedly wasn't really checking the number. She was searching, each time, for the one piece of information her mind most urgently wanted — has the falling stopped — and each unsuccessful check didn't just fail to provide relief, it actively extended the window of open-ended threat, which is precisely the condition Lazarus's research identifies as most corrosive to sustained coping.

There's a specific reason markets and falling asset values are especially well-suited to triggering this exact vulnerability, distinct from many other kinds of bad news. A single piece of clearly bad news — a rejection, a diagnosis, a layoff — however painful, usually arrives as a bounded, known event: it happened, it's specific, its scope is knowable even if its consequences take time to work out. A falling number, by contrast, is genuinely, structurally open-ended while it's happening — nobody, including the most sophisticated analysts in the world, can tell you with certainty where or when it stops, and that isn't a failure of information-gathering on your part; it's an accurate reflection of real uncertainty in the underlying situation. This means the floor-that-isn't-there feeling isn't irrational or a sign you're failing to gather enough information. It's an accurate perception of a genuinely unresolved situation, colliding with a mind that finds genuine unresolved situations specifically, disproportionately difficult to tolerate.

The entrepreneur's decision to take the worse-fitting contract makes complete sense once viewed through this lens: he wasn't optimizing for the best business outcome. He was optimizing to convert an intolerable, open-ended uncertainty into a known, bounded, even if worse, certainty — because a known bad outcome, appraisal theory suggests, is frequently easier to carry than an unresolved one, even when it's objectively the costlier choice. Selling in a panic often serves exactly this same function: it doesn't actually improve your financial position, and it may make it considerably worse, but it does something the falling number itself cannot do — it ends the open-endedness. Once you've sold, the loss is known, final, bounded. That's not a financial motive. It's a relief from uncertainty, purchased at a price the fear itself never asks you to calculate.

Lazarus's appraisal framework distinguishes two separate judgments the mind makes about any stressor, and it's worth naming both, because they explain why some open-ended situations feel survivable and others don't. The first judgment is primary appraisal: how serious is this, actually. The second is secondary appraisal: do I have the resources to cope with it. Critically, Lazarus's research found that emotional distress tracks the second judgment at least as strongly as the first — a genuinely serious situation that you believe you have the resources to handle can feel more manageable than a genuinely milder one where you believe your coping resources are inadequate. This is why the same falling number can devastate one investor and barely register with another holding a similar position: the difference often isn't the size of the decline, it's each person's secondary appraisal — whether they believe they have a plan, a timeline, a floor of some kind — adequate to the situation. The floor-that-isn't-there feeling isn't only about the market lacking a visible bottom. It's about the person, in that moment, not having ready access to a felt sense of their own coping resources, even when those resources genuinely exist on paper.

There's a useful, much older distinction worth bringing in here, from the economist Frank Knight, whose early-twentieth-century work drew a sharp line between two things people commonly lump together under the single word "risk." Knight distinguished risk, properly defined, as a situation where the range of possible outcomes and their probabilities are knowable, even if the specific outcome isn't — a coin flip, a well-understood insurance calculation — from what he called true uncertainty, where neither the full range of outcomes nor their likelihood can be reliably known in advance. This distinction matters enormously for the floor-that-isn't-there feeling, because it explains why "the market has always recovered eventually" — true, and statistically well-supported as a description of risk — doesn't actually soothe the feeling in the moment. The feeling isn't responding to risk in Knight's precise sense. It's responding to Knight's true uncertainty: the specific, unknowable question of how far this particular decline goes and how long it takes, which is a genuinely different, less tractable category of not-knowing than "the odds favor recovery over time." Knowing the odds favor you, in a domain of genuine Knightian uncertainty, is real and useful information — but it isn't the same as removing the uncertainty, and expecting it to feel the same is where a lot of well-intentioned reassurance quietly fails. This is worth dwelling on because it reframes what a good override actually needs to accomplish. An override that tries to convince you the situation is more knowable than it actually is will eventually fail, because it's making a claim reality won't consistently back up — some declines genuinely don't resolve the way past ones did, and pretending otherwise sets up a painful reckoning later. A better override, and the ones this chapter offers, works differently: it doesn't try to convert genuine uncertainty into false certainty. It tries to give you a stable place to stand — your timeline, your actual near-term needs, the plan you built in a calmer moment — that remains true regardless of how the genuine uncertainty eventually resolves. That's a more honest promise, and it turns out to be a more durable one too.

What it costs you

The direct cost is that selling specifically to end uncertainty, rather than because the underlying investment case has actually changed, converts a temporary, unrealized decline into a permanent, realized one, at precisely the moment — peak uncertainty, often close to peak fear across the broader market — when the price is likely to be least favorable. The relief you're buying by selling is real, and understandable, but it's relief from the feeling of open-endedness, not evidence that selling was the financially sound choice, and the two get confused constantly, because both produce the identical felt sense of "I feel better now."

The quieter cost is what happens to your tolerance for legitimate uncertainty over time. Each time an intolerable open-ended feeling gets resolved through an action that converts it into a known outcome, that pattern gets reinforced as the way you handle uncertainty in general — which makes it progressively harder to simply sit inside a genuinely unresolved situation the next time one arises, financial or otherwise, because you've built and repeatedly practiced a habit of resolving discomfort through action rather than through waiting.

This shows up well beyond investing — in careers, relationships, health decisions — anywhere an outcome is genuinely uncertain for a period of time before it resolves on its own.

There's a specific opportunity cost, too, worth naming honestly: the entrepreneur who took the worse-fitting contract didn't just accept a lower-quality client relationship. He also spent limited time and energy on a decision optimized for ending his own discomfort rather than for the actual health of the business, which meant that time wasn't available for the slower, harder work — refining the pitch, following up on the more promising but not-yet-closed leads — that might have addressed the underlying revenue gap more durably. Decisions made to end uncertainty tend to be the fastest available decision, not the best available one, and the two are so rarely the same thing that treating speed as a proxy for quality is, on its own, a quietly expensive habit.

There's a final cost worth naming, specific to how open-ended situations get resolved inside families rather than inside a single person's head: when one member of a household resolves their own intolerable uncertainty by taking unilateral action — moving joint funds, listing a shared property, canceling a shared contribution — without involving whoever else has a stake in the outcome, the relief they've purchased for themselves often creates a new, second-order uncertainty for everyone else affected by the decision, who now has to cope with an outcome they had no part in shaping. The retired couple in this chapter's opening scene at least made their decision together. Not every open-ended-uncertainty panic is this considerate; plenty happen alone, at a keyboard, late at night, and are only discovered by everyone else the following morning, which converts one person's private intolerance of not-knowing into a shared, retroactive uncertainty for the whole household about what else might get decided the same way next time.

There's a fourth cost worth naming, one that showed up plainly in the man waiting out the two quarters of layoff uncertainty: the toll of sustained, unresolved threat isn't confined to the eventual financial decision. It shows up first, and often more severely, in sleep, concentration, and the ordinary functioning of daily life, well before any money actually changes hands. Lazarus's own research on prolonged, unpredictable stressors documented exactly this pattern — that the anticipation of an unresolved threat frequently produces more measurable strain than the threat's eventual, known resolution, meaning a portion of this cost is paid in full regardless of whether you eventually act on the fear or not. Liquidating the account didn't spare him this cost. He paid it in full during the four months of not knowing, and then paid a second, separate cost in the growth the liquidated account missed — two bills for a single uncertain season, when a felt sense of a floor might have reduced the first without requiring the second at all.

The overrides

Name the uncertainty explicitly as the thing you're reacting to, not the number itself. When you notice the urge to check repeatedly, or the pull toward an action that would "just make this stop," pause and ask directly: am I reacting to how bad this actually is, or to not knowing when it stops? These require different responses, and naming which one is actually driving the urgency is often enough, on its own, to reduce its grip somewhat — because an identified, named source of distress is generally more manageable than an unnamed one.

The Move: replace repeated checking with a single, scheduled check and a written "known unknowns" list. Rather than checking an unpredictable number on an unpredictable schedule — which repeatedly reopens the open-endedness — commit to checking it once, at a set time you choose, and in between checks, write out explicitly what you do and don't know: "I don't know when this stops. I do know my original timeline. I do know this account isn't money I need in the next several years." This doesn't manufacture false certainty about the market. It gives your mind a genuine, honest floor to stand on — not "the losses will stop here," but "here is what remains true and known, regardless of what the number does next" — which is a real answer to appraisal theory's actual requirement, even though it isn't the answer the anxious mind is originally asking for.

Distinguish a bounded risk you already accepted from a new, unbounded one. Before reacting to an open-ended feeling, ask whether the range of outcomes was already something you considered and accepted when you first made this decision — most long-term financial plans are built with significant temporary declines already priced into the expected range — or whether something has genuinely, structurally changed the range of possible outcomes. Often the falling itself feels newly unbounded, when in fact it's still comfortably inside a range you already planned for; making that comparison explicit restores a floor that was there all along, just obscured by the feeling of the moment.

Practice sitting inside smaller uncertainties on purpose, away from money. Because intolerance of uncertainty is a general capacity, not one specific to finance, deliberately practicing staying calm inside small, low-stakes unresolved situations — an unanswered message, an ambiguous outcome at work — builds a more general tolerance that transfers, at least partially, to the higher-stakes version. This isn't a quick fix, but it's a real, buildable capacity, not a fixed trait.

Strengthen your secondary appraisal on purpose, before the uncertainty arrives. Since distress tracks your felt sense of having adequate resources at least as strongly as the actual severity of the situation, build and rehearse a concrete, written answer to "what are my coping resources here" before you need it — your actual timeline, the actual portion of your total plan this specific account represents, the actual steps you'd take if the decline continued further. Rehearsing this answer in a calm moment makes it far more accessible during an anxious one, when constructing it from scratch is exactly the kind of slow, deliberate task the alarmed mind is least capable of doing well.

Separate Knightian risk from genuine uncertainty explicitly, in writing, before deciding which one you're facing. When a decision feels paralyzed by not-knowing, write down, specifically: is this a situation where the range of outcomes and rough odds are actually knowable (Knight's risk), or one where they genuinely aren't (Knight's uncertainty)? Most financial market declines are closer to the first category than they feel in the moment — the range of historical outcomes for a diversified position over a multi-year horizon is, in fact, reasonably well understood, even though the specific path to get there isn't. Naming which category you're actually in keeps you from treating a knowable-odds situation as if it offered no information at all.

Give the unresolved situation an honest, explicit re-check date, out loud. Part of what makes open-endedness so corrosive is the sense that the not-knowing could, in principle, continue forever. Counter this directly by setting a specific, calendared point — not a promise that the situation will be resolved by then, but a committed moment when you will deliberately reassess, with whatever information exists at that time, rather than reassessing continuously, every hour, in a way that only deepens the sense of open-endedness. A bounded period of not-knowing, with a real date attached, is measurably easier to tolerate than an unbounded one, even when the underlying uncertainty hasn't actually changed at all.

The falling itself was never the whole threat — not knowing when it stops was. Build a floor out of what you already know is still true, and stand on that instead of the number.

Chapter 7 — The Relief That Costs You Twice

Why Selling Feels Like Winning, Even When It's the Worse Move

The instant after she sells, before any confirmation screen has even loaded, she feels something unmistakable: relief, sudden and total, like a held breath finally released. Her shoulders drop. The tightness in her chest, which had been building for two days, eases almost immediately. For a few minutes, she genuinely feels like she's done something right — competent, decisive, protective. It will be days before the actual financial consequences of the sale become clear, and weeks before she'll have any real read on whether it was, in fact, the correct call. But the relief doesn't wait for any of that. It arrives instantly, attached not to the quality of the decision but simply to the fact that a decision was made at all, ending a period of unbearable, anxious waiting. The relief is real. It is also completely uninformative about whether selling was actually the right choice — and because it feels so much like being right, it's easy to mistake the one for the other.

A second scene, entirely different in scale and setting: a man managing a modest inheritance he received two years earlier, watching it lose value during a difficult stretch, who finally, after several sleepless nights, moves the entire remaining amount into something he considers completely safe — plain, boring, guaranteed not to move. The relief he feels afterward is enormous, disproportionate, almost euphoric, and he describes it to his wife that evening as "finally being able to breathe again." What he doesn't examine closely, in that moment or for a long while afterward, is that the relief arrived the second the decision was made and the account was moved — well before any information had arrived about whether the original investment would have recovered, whether the "safe" alternative he chose would actually meet his longer-term goals, or whether he'd simply traded a temporary discomfort for a permanent reduction in what the money could eventually become. The relief wasn't a verdict on the decision. It was a response to the waiting finally being over.

A third, smaller scene shows the same mechanism at a scale most people will recognize instantly. A woman spends a tense morning debating whether to cancel a modest recurring investment contribution during a rough week for her portfolio, going back and forth for nearly an hour, before finally clicking cancel — not after resolving the underlying question of whether continuing to invest during a downturn actually made sense, which is the harder, slower question she never quite answers, but simply because the back-and-forth itself had become exhausting. The relief she feels the moment she clicks isn't relief about having made a good decision. It's relief that the deciding is over. She recognizes this herself, hours later, with a kind of rueful clarity: she didn't conclude anything. She just got tired of the question and let the click answer it for her.

A fourth scene shows the same relief mechanism operating in reverse timing, worth including because it demonstrates the relief doesn't even require completing the action — sometimes the decision to act is enough to trigger it early. A man deciding, mid-afternoon, to sell a long-held position the moment markets reopen the next morning, spends that entire evening in a state of calm he hasn't felt in days, sleeping well for the first time that week, describing the feeling to his wife as having "finally made a decision." Nothing has actually changed yet — the position is still fully held, still fully exposed to whatever happens overnight, and a meaningful piece of news could arrive before the market opens that would make the planned sale look premature or unnecessary. But the relief doesn't wait for the actual transaction. It arrives the moment the decision crystallizes, because the decision itself is what ends the anxious deliberation — the actual sale, the next morning, is almost an afterthought, executed on autopilot to complete what the relief had already treated as settled the night before. This matters because it shows how early in the process the trap actually closes: by the time you're watching the confirmation screen, as in the chapter's opening scene, the real decision — and the real, misleading relief — may have already happened hours or even a full day earlier, with no chance left for new information to intervene.

What's actually happening

This pattern draws on a body of research into how the brain processes anxiety, action, and reward, and one of the clearest, most relevant threads within it involves the role of action itself

— not outcome, action — in reducing perceived threat. A substantial line of research on anxiety and coping has found that taking action, almost any action, during a period of anxious uncertainty tends to reduce subjective distress measurably, even when the action taken doesn't actually improve the underlying situation and, in some studied cases, makes it objectively worse. The relief isn't coming from having solved the problem. It's coming from having done something in response to it, which the nervous system registers as a form of regained control, regardless of whether control was actually regained in any way that matters to the outcome.

This connects to well-established findings on the neurobiology of relief and reward: the cessation of a stress response is itself processed by reward-related circuitry in ways that can feel similar to a positive, appetitive reward, even though nothing good has actually happened — the stress has simply stopped. This is sometimes discussed under the broader banner of negative reinforcement, a concept with deep roots in behavioral psychology: a behavior that ends an aversive state gets reinforced, made more likely to recur, purely by virtue of ending that state, independent of whether the behavior produced any positive outcome beyond the ending itself. Selling under anxiety functions exactly this way. The behavior — selling — ends the aversive state of anxious waiting, and the relief that follows reinforces the behavior, teaching the nervous system that "selling when anxious" is an effective, rewarded strategy, regardless of what the sale actually did to the underlying financial position.

This is worth stating plainly because of how deceptive it is from the inside: the relief you feel after a panic sale is not your intuition correctly recognizing a good decision. It is a completely separate system — the one that rewards the ending of distress — firing in response to the ending of your distress, which happens to have been accomplished, in this instance, through a financial transaction. If you'd ended the same anxious feeling by closing the laptop and going for a walk without selling anything, a milder version of the identical relief mechanism would likely have fired too, because the relief tracks the reduction of anxious arousal, not the financial merit of what caused it. The trouble is that only one of those two paths —

selling — also happens to lock in a financial outcome, and the relief, arriving instantly and powerfully, makes that path feel not just emotionally easier but actually correct, blending two entirely separate questions — "does this feel better" and "was this the right call" — into one indistinguishable feeling.

The man moving his inheritance to "something safe" experienced this with particular intensity because the relief was compounded by a second, related mechanism: the completeness of the move. A partial reduction in exposure would have left some ongoing uncertainty, and therefore some ongoing anxiety, still active. A complete move to something he perceived as fully safe ended the uncertainty entirely, which produced a correspondingly larger relief response — not because it was a correspondingly better decision, but because the relief mechanism scales with how thoroughly the aversive state has been ended, not with how sound the underlying choice was.

There's a further layer worth naming, because it explains why the relief can feel not just calming but actively good, almost triumphant, rather than merely neutral. Anxious anticipation — the specific state of waiting for a bad outcome you can't control or predict — is itself metabolically and psychologically costly to sustain; the body spends real resources staying in a state of heightened alert over an extended period. When that state ends, the relief isn't just the absence of a negative. It registers, physiologically, as its own kind of positive event, sometimes described in the stress literature as a rebound effect, where the sharp drop in stress hormones produces a felt sense of well-being that can temporarily exceed the person's actual baseline mood before the anxious period began. This is part of why the woman at her kitchen table and the man moving his inheritance both describe the moment after selling in language that sounds closer to triumph than mere relief — "finally being able to breathe again" isn't a modest description of stress ending. It's a genuine high, chemically real, and entirely disconnected from whether the transaction that produced it was financially sound.

There's a related, well-documented finding worth adding from the research of economist George Loewenstein, whose work on what he termed visceral factors examined how intense emotional or physiological states — fear, craving, pain, anxious arousal among them — systematically distort decision-making in ways that are predictable but very difficult to correct for in the moment they're happening. Loewenstein's research found that people under the influence of a strong visceral state consistently underestimate how much that state is shaping their judgment, and separately, tend to badly mispredict how they'll feel and what they'll want once the visceral state has passed — a gap he studied extensively under the broader heading of affective forecasting. Applied here: the man who decides the evening before to sell isn't making a cool, forward-looking assessment of his actual financial situation. He's making a decision almost entirely organized around ending a visceral state — anxious arousal — that Loewenstein's research says he is, in that exact moment, systematically unable to see clearly enough to discount. The decision feels like foresight. It is, more accurately, a visceral state finding the fastest available exit, with the actual financial reasoning constructed, as Chapter 4 described, well after the fact.

It's worth adding one further distinction Loewenstein's research draws out clearly, because it explains why simply "waiting for the feeling to pass" is a more reliable override than most people expect it to be, even though it can feel, in the moment, like a flimsy piece of advice. Visceral states, by their nature, are time-limited — the specific intensity of acute anxious arousal is not designed to sustain itself indefinitely, and it reliably softens with time, even without any deliberate intervention. This means the affective-forecasting error runs in a genuinely predictable direction: people reliably overestimate how long a current visceral state will last and how it will still feel hours or days later, which means a decision deferred past the acute window is, on average, a decision made by a meaningfully calmer and more accurate version of the same person. The advice to "wait it out" isn't vague comfort. It's a direct, evidence-based countermeasure to a specific, well-documented forecasting error.

What it costs you

The direct financial cost is what you'd expect: relief-driven decisions, evaluated purely on how much anxiety they end rather than on their actual merit, systematically favor complete, immediate, drastic action over measured, partial, well-timed action — because complete and immediate is what produces the biggest relief. This tends to push people toward selling everything rather than trimming a position, toward moving to the most conservative option available rather than a more moderate adjustment that might have better served their actual goals, simply because the more drastic move produces the larger, more satisfying relief signal, independent of whether it's the more appropriate financial response to the actual situation.

The subtler, more corrosive cost is what this does to your ability to trust your own sense of having made a good decision. Because the relief feels so much like being right, and arrives so immediately, it tends to short-circuit the more careful, delayed evaluation that would actually tell you whether the decision was sound. People who panic-sell often report feeling, in the moment right after, unusually confident and clear — not confused or regretful, but genuinely relieved and settled — which makes it considerably harder to catch the decision while there's still time to reconsider, because every internal signal available in that moment is telling you that you just did the right thing, when what you actually did was end an uncomfortable feeling through the fastest available method.

A third cost worth naming is what this pattern teaches you about which problems deserve financial action in the first place. If selling reliably produces relief regardless of its actual merit, the nervous system learns, over repeated instances, that financial action is a generally effective way to manage anxiety of any kind — not just anxiety directly caused by a financial situation. This can widen over time into a habit of reaching for a financial lever whenever anxiety rises for any reason, financial or not, simply because it's a lever that reliably produces the specific relief the body is seeking, whether or not it's actually the right tool for whatever is actually driving the anxiety that day.

There's a fourth cost worth naming, because it shows up specifically in how people describe these decisions to others, long after the fact, in a way that quietly recruits new believers into the same pattern. Someone who panic-sold and later felt an enormous, genuine wave of relief tends, months or years down the line, to describe the whole episode using the language of good judgment rather than anxious action — not out of dishonesty, but because Chapter 4's story-building machinery and this chapter's relief mechanism reinforce each other over time, each one making the other's version of events feel more solid. The result is that the people most likely to speak confidently, in social settings, about "trusting your gut" during a downturn are disproportionately the people whose gut led them somewhere costly, dressed up afterward in the unearned authority that strong relief and a smoothed-over story combine to produce. Anyone listening to that confident account, without knowing to ask what the relief was actually responding to, absorbs a model of good decision-making that is, underneath the confident delivery, closer to a cautionary tale.

The overrides

Name the relief for what it is, immediately, out loud if possible. The moment you notice relief following a financial decision made under anxiety, say directly: "This relief is about the waiting being over, not about whether this was the right decision." This doesn't erase the relief — you can't reason a feeling away — but it prevents the relief from being silently misfiled as evidence that the decision itself was sound, which is the actual danger, not the feeling.

The Move: separate the anxiety-reduction action from the financial action, and take the former without the latter first. The next time anxious waiting becomes unbearable, deliberately take a genuinely anxiety-reducing action that has no financial consequence at all — a walk, a phone call to someone you trust, physical movement, anything that engages the same stress-response system without touching your account — before allowing yourself to make any financial decision. If the urge to sell remains just as strong after the non-financial relief has been achieved, that's meaningful information: it suggests there may be a genuine underlying reason to reconsider your position, worth examining calmly. If the urge fades once the anxiety itself has been addressed through a non-financial channel, that's equally meaningful: it confirms the urge to sell was really an urge to end distress, wearing a financial decision as its method.

Delay the financial action specifically until after the relief has been achieved by other means. Build this as a standing rule: no financial decision made under high anxiety is executed until you've first done something to reduce the anxiety that doesn't involve the decision itself. This breaks the fused link between "ending distress" and "selling," which is the entire mechanism this chapter describes, and it lets any remaining, post-relief urge to sell be evaluated on its actual financial merits rather than on how urgently it promises to make the discomfort stop.

Track the feeling and the outcome separately, and check them against each other later. After any significant financial decision made under stress, write down, at the time, how relieved you felt — a simple number, one to ten, nothing elaborate. Weeks later, once the actual outcome is clearer, compare the two: did the relief predict a good decision, or did it simply predict the end of your own anxious waiting? Doing this consistently, over several decisions, builds a personal, honest track record that makes the disconnect between the two impossible to keep ignoring.

Watch for the pattern in how you narrate past decisions, not just how you make new ones. Because the story-building and relief mechanisms reinforce each other over time, periodically revisit how you describe your own past financial decisions to other people, especially the ones you tell with the most confidence. Ask whether the confident version matches a contemporaneous record, or whether it has quietly absorbed the polish that strong relief tends to apply to a story in hindsight. This is slower, retrospective work compared to the other overrides in this chapter, but it interrupts a specific, compounding harm: the confident retelling that recruits your own future self, and sometimes other people, into repeating a pattern you never actually examined honestly.

Expect the rebound high, and discount it on purpose. Knowing in advance that ending a period of anxious waiting produces a genuine, chemically real high — not just calm, but something closer to euphoria — lets you treat an unusually elated, triumphant feeling after a financial decision as a predictable side effect of the relief itself, rather than as independent confirmation that the decision was wise. The bigger and more triumphant the feeling, the more worth discounting it is, precisely because its size tracks how much anxiety just ended, not how sound the choice was.

Treat the moment of deciding, not just the moment of executing, as the point of real risk. Because relief can arrive as soon as a decision crystallizes — sometimes well before it's actually carried out — build your delay rule (from earlier in this chapter) around the decision itself, not around the transaction. If you notice you've quietly "decided" to sell tomorrow, or next week, treat that decision as the trigger for your waiting period to begin, rather than waiting until you're about to click through, by which point the relief has often already done its work and the actual click has become a formality.

Relief tells you the waiting is over. It does not tell you the decision was right — check the second thing separately, because the first one will always feel like enough on its own.

Chapter 8 — The Return Trip

Why Buying Back In Costs More Than the Panic That Sent You Out

He watches, over the following weeks, as the exact position he sold in a panic climbs back past the price he sold it at, then keeps climbing. He doesn't buy back in right away. He tells himself, at first, that he's waiting for a pullback, a better entry point, some confirmation that the recovery is real and not a temporary bounce before another leg down — reasonable-sounding language that, if he's honest with himself later, is really just fear wearing a new outfit, the same alarm system that told him to sell now telling him, with equal confidence, not to buy back in yet. He watches it climb further. Eventually, well after the price has moved meaningfully past where he sold, the fear of missing the recovery entirely becomes louder than the fear of buying back in at a bad moment, and he buys back in — at a price notably higher than where he sold, having paid, in effect, twice: once in the original panic-driven loss, and again in the higher price required to re-enter after watching the recovery happen without him.

A different version of the same round trip, on a longer timeline: a woman who sold a piece of property during a period of acute anxiety about a downturn in her local market, convinced that prices had further to fall and that getting out now, even at a loss relative to what she'd hoped to get, was the responsible move. She rents for the following two years, watching, with a specific kind of quiet dread she doesn't discuss with anyone, as property values in the same market not only recover but climb well past where they were when she sold — while she has spent those two years paying rent that, combined with the loss she took on the original sale, adds up to a genuinely significant sum, far more than the modest additional loss she would have absorbed by simply staying and riding out the downturn she was so afraid of. When she finally decides to buy again, in year three, she's re-entering a market at a considerably higher price than the one she fled, having paid, across the full round trip, a cost far larger than the single bad afternoon that originally frightened her.

A third, quieter version involves no re-entry at all, which is its own kind of round trip. A man who sold a long-held stake in a family business during a period of acute conflict with a co-owner, convinced the whole venture was collapsing, watches from the outside for years afterward as the business not only survives the conflict but grows well past where it stood when he left. He never buys back in — there's no clean mechanism to do so, and the relationship that would make it possible was part of what the original panic damaged. His round trip isn't a repurchase at a higher price. It's a permanent, compounding absence from something that kept growing without him, and the fact that there's no single transaction to point to as "the cost" makes it, if anything, easier to underestimate and harder to learn from.

It's worth pausing on what connects all four of these scenes before moving into the mechanism itself, because the connecting thread is easy to miss if you focus only on the size of the dollar figures involved. In every case, the person's second decision — the decision to stay out, to wait, to hesitate, to never return — was treated, by the person making it, as fundamentally different in kind from the first, panic-driven decision to leave. The designer converting her position back to cash after a rough quarter didn't experience that as a second panic; she experienced it as prudent damage control. The man watching the recovery happen without him didn't experience his hesitation as fear; he experienced it as discipline. This is precisely the trap. The round trip isn't two separate decisions, one emotional and one rational. It's the same emotional system, still running, simply having changed its specific verdict from "get out" to "don't get back in yet" — a change in direction, not a change in kind.

A fourth scene shows the round trip taking a shorter, faster form, useful because it demonstrates the same pattern doesn't require years to do real damage — it can complete itself inside a single difficult month. A freelance graphic designer, panicking during a slow stretch of client work, converts a modest emergency fund she'd built specifically to smooth over exactly this kind of slow stretch into a more "growth-oriented" position, reasoning, in the anxious moment, that the emergency fund's low return is "wasting an opportunity" she should be capturing instead — a rationalization that has nothing to do with why she built the fund in the first place. Three weeks later, a genuinely slow month arrives, exactly the kind the fund existed to cushion, and she's forced to sell the growth-oriented position at a loss, at a bad moment, to cover ordinary expenses — converting a short-term dip into a locked-in loss, and leaving herself with less than she started with, all inside a single financial quarter. The round trip here isn't a re-entry at a higher price months later. It's a complete cycle — safe to risky to forced-sale — compressed into weeks, driven by the same underlying discomfort with an account that wasn't actively "doing" anything, dressed up as an opportunity rather than named as what it actually was: impatience with stillness.

What's actually happening

This pattern is sometimes described in behavioral finance research as the behavior gap — a term used to describe the well-documented, empirically studied difference between the returns an investment itself produces over time and the actual returns real investors experience, a gap driven substantially by the timing of when people buy and sell relative to their own emotional state rather than relative to any underlying change in value. Researchers studying investor behavior, including work associated with economist Terrance Odean examining the trading patterns of individual investors, have found a consistent pattern: individual investors, on average, tend to sell after price drops and buy after price recoveries — precisely the reverse of what a strategy focused on value would recommend, and precisely the pattern this chapter's two scenes describe. This isn't a matter of a few unlucky individuals making isolated mistakes. It's a broad, statistically consistent pattern, and its consistency is exactly what makes it worth taking seriously as a predictable feature of how fear and relief interact with financial decision-making, not a random string of individual bad luck.

The reason the round trip is so expensive, specifically, deserves its own explanation, because it isn't simply "selling low and buying high" as an abstract idea — it's driven by the same alarm system operating in both directions, with a specific, asymmetric timing built in. The panic that triggers the initial sale fires fast, often at or near the point of maximum visible fear, which is frequently close to a low point, precisely because that's when the threat signal is loudest. The relief and confidence needed to buy back in, by contrast, requires the alarm to quiet down first — and the alarm doesn't quiet down until enough time has passed, and enough of the recovery has already visibly happened, for the situation to feel safe again. This isn't a coincidental design flaw. It's the same threat-detection logic working correctly on its own terms: don't return to a place that recently registered as dangerous until you have substantial evidence it's genuinely safe again. That logic serves you well when the "place" is a den that recently had a predator in it. Applied to a market, it guarantees that the fear-driven sale happens near the bottom and the relief-driven re-entry happens well after a meaningful recovery is already underway — a structurally, reliably expensive round trip, not a matter of bad luck striking twice.

There's an additional psychological layer worth naming: research on regret and decision-making has found that people are often more troubled by losses that result from action — a decision they actively made — than by equivalent or even larger losses that result from inaction, a pattern sometimes discussed under the broader umbrella of action-inaction asymmetries in regret. This helps explain the specific hesitation both figures in this chapter's scenes show before re-entering: having already taken one costly action (selling), the prospect of taking a second action (buying back in) that might also turn out to be badly timed feels more threatening than simply continuing to do nothing, even though continuing to do nothing — staying out of the market, staying out of the housing market — was, in both cases, actively accumulating its own separate, ongoing cost the entire time. Inaction doesn't feel like a decision in the moment, even when it functions as one with real, ongoing consequences.

This asymmetry has a name worth knowing on its own, because it shows up well beyond the specific decision to re-enter: economists and psychologists studying it have described a related pattern often called the status quo bias, a general preference for the current state of affairs — whatever it happens to be — over any alternative, even when the alternative would objectively serve the person better. Once "being out of the market" becomes the current state, simply by virtue of the original sale having already happened, that state acquires a kind of default gravity it wouldn't have had if the person were choosing fresh, from scratch, whether to be in or out. This is part of why the man in the first scene keeps waiting for "one more signal" rather than simply re-evaluating his position on its merits: the sold position has already become the status quo, and the status quo, once established, resists correction independent of whether it was ever the right place to be. The original panic doesn't just cause one bad decision. It quietly resets the baseline against which every future decision gets compared, and that new, lower baseline is much harder to notice than the original, dramatic sale ever was.

There's a closely related, extensively studied pattern worth naming here, identified by researchers Hersh Shefrin and Meir Statman and generally called the disposition effect: the well-documented tendency of investors to sell winning positions too early, locking in modest gains prematurely, while holding losing positions too long, waiting for a loss to "come back" before they're willing to part with it. At first glance this looks like the opposite pattern from the one this chapter describes, but the two are, underneath, driven by closely related psychology. Shefrin and Statman's research traced the disposition effect to the same reference-point-dependent thinking that shapes loss aversion — people evaluate a position not against its objective merit today, but against the price they originally paid, and that anchor distorts both directions of the round trip described in this chapter. The freelancer selling her emergency fund never framed it as "locking in a loss relative to a reference point" — but the reluctance to buy back in after a panic sale, described earlier in this chapter, is disposition-effect thinking running in reverse: the sale price becomes a new anchor, and re-entering above it feels like "paying more than it's worth," even when the current price is a perfectly fair reflection of a position that has simply recovered. The anchor, once set by the panic, quietly organizes every future decision around itself, regardless of whether it was ever a meaningful number to anchor to in the first place.

It's worth adding one further piece of Odean's broader research here, because it complicates a natural assumption readers might otherwise make: that the fix for a panic-driven round trip is simply trading less often, or hesitating more before any single move. Odean's work on individual investor behavior found that excessive trading itself, independent of timing, tends to erode returns — investors who traded most frequently, across the population he studied, systematically underperformed those who traded least, largely because trading costs and repeated bad timing compound against the frequent trader in ways that patience alone doesn't cost. This matters for the round trip specifically because it means the damage isn't confined to the one bad sale and the one bad re-entry described in this chapter's scenes. A person prone to this pattern is often prone to it repeatedly, in smaller version, across many separate decisions — each one a miniature round trip, each one shaving a little more off the total than standing still would have. The chapter's scenes describe the dramatic version. Odean's broader research suggests the quieter, more frequent version may be doing comparable damage over a longer stretch of time, simply distributed across more transactions and harder to see as a single, nameable event.

What it costs you

The direct cost is the round trip itself, measured plainly: the gap between the price sold at and the price re-entered at, which — in a pattern this consistent across real investor behavior — is very often a meaningfully worse price than either the original sale price or a simple, uninterrupted hold would have produced. This cost is frequently larger than the cost of the initial panic-driven sale alone, because it compounds the original mistake with a second, structurally near-inevitable one, driven by the same alarm system now working in reverse.

The quieter cost, present in both scenes, is the extended period of limbo between the sale and the re-entry — months or years spent neither fully invested nor fully at peace, watching from outside, alternately hoping for a pullback and dreading being left behind, a genuinely uncomfortable state that gets rarely acknowledged as a cost in its own right, separate from the eventual dollar figure. The woman renting for two years wasn't simply waiting patiently. She was living inside an ongoing, low-grade version of the same anxiety that triggered the original sale, now aimed at a different target — not "will this fall further" but "will I miss the recovery entirely" — which is its own real, measurable toll on the years she spent carrying it.

There's a compounding cost in the man's story worth naming as well: the family business he left behind, in his ongoing absence, has had to make decisions and build relationships without his contribution, some of which shaped how the business grew in directions he had no input into and now has no claim on. The round trip in a case like this isn't only financial. It's a permanent redirection of a piece of his own history, and the cost of that redirection compounds every year he stays outside it, in ways no single dollar figure ever fully captures.

There's a specific cost worth naming that applies across all four scenes in this chapter, easy to miss because it doesn't show up as a single dramatic figure: the round trip doesn't just cost the difference between the sale price and the re-entry price. It also costs whatever the money would have earned had it stayed invested the entire time, including through the very decline that triggered the original panic — a cost sometimes called opportunity cost, which compounds silently in the background regardless of whether anyone is tracking it. A position sold in fear and bought back later doesn't just re-enter at a worse price. It also missed every dividend, every reinvestment, every day of compounding that happened during the months or years it sat in cash, waiting for the fear to pass. This piece of the cost never appears on any single statement as a labeled line item, which is exactly why it's the piece most people never fully reckon with, even when they're honest with themselves about everything else the round trip cost them. Add to this the psychological cost of the limbo period itself — measured not in dollars but in the specific, ongoing toll of a mind that's never quite settled, alternately hoping for a pullback and dreading being left behind — and the true cost of any single panic-driven exit is almost always larger, once fully accounted for, than the number that shows up on the day of the original sale. The sale is the visible, dated event. The round trip is the real cost, and it rarely announces itself with a single number the way the original panic did.

The overrides

Recognize re-entry hesitation as the same alarm system, not a separate, more careful decision. When you notice yourself waiting for "more confirmation" or "a better entry point" after a panic-driven sale, ask directly whether this caution is actually well-reasoned, or whether it's the identical threat-detection system that triggered the original sale, now applied in reverse to the decision to return. The language will sound more careful and considered than the original panic did. The underlying mechanism, more often than not, is the same one.

The Move: build a pre-committed re-entry plan at the moment you sell, not months later while watching the recovery happen. If you sell a position under stress, and you genuinely believe, once calmer, that some version of that position still belongs in your plan, write a specific re-entry plan immediately — a price, a date, or a fixed schedule — while you're making the sale, rather than leaving the re-entry decision to be made later, under whatever emotional state happens to be active by then. This removes the second decision from the same compromised, emotionally-driven process that produced the first one, giving you, in effect, a version of yourself from before the panic making the re-entry call in advance.

Weigh the cost of the round trip against the cost of the original fear, honestly, before waiting further. When deciding whether to re-enter, calculate, as concretely as you can, what the delay itself is costing — in a rising market, in accumulating rent, in whatever the specific parallel is for your situation — and weigh that explicitly against the fear driving the hesitation. This doesn't guarantee a better-timed decision, since no one can time these things reliably, but it makes the cost of waiting visible and concrete, rather than allowing it to remain an invisible, unmeasured cost that the fear of a second mistake obscures entirely.

Treat "staying out" as an active decision with its own ongoing cost, not a safe default. Reframe continued inaction explicitly, in your own mind, as a choice you're actively making and actively paying for — not a neutral pause where nothing is happening. This directly counters the action-inaction asymmetry described above, which quietly treats inaction as free simply because it doesn't feel like a decision.

Ask whether you'd choose the current position fresh, with no history attached. To counter the status quo bias directly, periodically ask a specific, deliberately history-free question: if I were starting completely fresh today, with no memory of having sold, would I choose to be out of this position at this price? If the honest answer is no, the only thing keeping you out is the gravity of the status quo the original panic created, not any ongoing, independent judgment that being out is actually correct.

Identify your own anchor price explicitly, and then deliberately ignore it. Because the disposition effect shows anchoring works in both directions, name the specific price you sold at or bought at, in writing, and then ask directly: if this number didn't exist — if I had genuinely no memory of it — would today's price still look reasonable on its own terms? The anchor doesn't disappear just because you've named it, but naming it explicitly is what makes it possible to ask the question underneath it, which the anchor otherwise answers silently and automatically, without ever being examined.

The panic sends you out near the bottom and the relief brings you back near the top — the same alarm runs both trips, and only a plan made before either one can interrupt the pattern.

Chapter 9 — The Body That Remembers

Why the Second Panic Comes Faster Than the First

The first time it happened, it took a genuinely severe, headline-worthy downturn to trigger the flight response — a real, significant, widely-covered event, the kind that made the news, the kind that, in hindsight, plenty of careful people found unsettling. The second time, two years later, it took considerably less: a smaller, more ordinary dip, nowhere near the scale of the first event, and yet the same full-body alarm fired, at close to the same intensity, in a fraction of the time it took the first time around. He noticed this himself, with a kind of detached surprise, sitting at his desk watching a moderate decline that, by any reasonable measure, was well within normal market behavior — and feeling his chest tighten with an urgency that felt exactly like the first time, despite the actual situation being considerably less severe. It wasn't that he'd become more anxious about money generally. It was that the specific pathway from "falling number" to "flee now" had been used once, successfully, in the sense that it had ended his distress quickly, and a used pathway is a strengthened pathway — faster and more available the second time, regardless of whether the underlying situation actually warranted the same response.

A second scene, on a different timeline: a woman who panic-sold a piece of a small business she co-owned during a genuinely frightening early period, watching a key client relationship collapse unexpectedly and fearing, in that moment, that the business itself might be failing. She sold her stake at a real loss, driven by an authentic, if ultimately overcorrected, fear. Years later, running an entirely different, unrelated venture, she notices something troubling: the first sign of any friction with a client — a slightly delayed payment, a mildly critical piece of feedback — now produces a disproportionate, fast wave of the identical dread she felt during the original crisis, even though the current situation, examined honestly, bears little resemblance to the one that originally frightened her. Her business partner notices it too, gently, more than once — that she seems to go from calm to catastrophic in a matter of minutes, over problems that, to him, look like ordinary friction rather than emergencies. She isn't imagining a new threat each time. She's re-experiencing, at high speed, a version of the original one, triggered by inputs that only loosely resemble it.

A third scene shows the same widened pathway passing between people rather than simply persisting inside one, worth including because it reveals how a single household panic can seed a faster trigger in someone who wasn't even the one who panicked the first time. A teenager, present in the room the day her parents sold a chunk of the family's investments during a frightening stretch — not understanding the specifics, but absorbing, at close range, the tension in the house, the raised voices, the sense of emergency that lingered for days afterward — grows into an adult with a strikingly fast, disproportionate flinch response to her own, much smaller financial setbacks, years before she has any comparable personal history of her own to explain it. Her own first "panic," in her twenties, arrives shockingly fast and hits with an intensity that seems, on its face, mismatched to her limited financial experience — until you account for the fact that the pathway wasn't built entirely from her own direct experience. Some of it was absorbed secondhand, watching people she depended on go through the identical sequence years earlier, at an age when she had no framework yet for distinguishing "this is a serious household emergency" from "this is what financial stress generally looks like." The sensitized pathway this chapter describes doesn't require you to have lived through the original panic yourself. Sometimes you inherit an already-widened road.

What's actually happening

This pattern draws on a well-established finding in the study of fear and learning: sensitization, a process in which a strong initial response to a threat lowers the threshold required to trigger a similar response in the future, making subsequent reactions faster, more intense, or triggered by weaker, less specific cues than the ones that produced the original response. This sits alongside, and is closely related to, classical fear conditioning — the broad, extensively studied process by which a nervous system, once it has strongly associated a specific pattern of cues with danger, becomes primed to respond to that same pattern, or even a rough approximation of it, with increasing speed and decreasing need for the full original context to be present. The first panic doesn't just resolve and disappear once it's over. It leaves behind a strengthened, faster pathway — the neural equivalent of a shortcut that's been walked once, successfully, and is now easier to find and use again.

This connects directly to the low-road pathway discussed back in Chapter 1, in Joseph LeDoux's research on fast, amygdala-driven threat processing: each time that low road fires and produces a fast, effective-feeling response — meaning, from the nervous system's perspective, the action successfully ended a period of felt threat — the pathway gets reinforced, made more accessible, more likely to fire again with less provocation next time. This is not a design flaw specific to financial panic. It's the same basic mechanism that makes a person who's been in one car accident more reactive to sudden braking for years afterward, or a person who experienced one bad medical scare more attentive, sometimes disproportionately so, to minor physical symptoms going forward. The nervous system, having learned once that a certain pattern of signals preceded real danger, becomes appropriately — from its own perspective — more vigilant about that pattern in the future. The trouble, as in the earlier chapters, is that this vigilance doesn't discriminate well between a genuine repeat of the original threat and a much milder situation that merely shares a surface resemblance to it.

This is precisely why the man's second panic, triggered by a considerably smaller dip, fired with nearly the same intensity as the first: the pathway wasn't being asked to evaluate the current situation on its own merits. It was being asked whether the current inputs resembled the pattern it had already learned to treat as dangerous, and a falling number, any falling number, resembled that pattern closely enough to trigger a strengthened, faster version of the original response. The business owner's disproportionate reaction to ordinary client friction works the same way — her nervous system isn't overreacting randomly. It's applying a well-learned, appropriately-calibrated-to-the-original-event response to a new situation that shares just enough surface features with the original crisis to activate the same strengthened pathway, at a speed and intensity calibrated to a threat level the current situation doesn't actually contain.

There is real hope embedded in this same research, and it's worth stating clearly, because sensitization is not a one-way, permanent ratchet. The same broad body of research on fear conditioning has also extensively documented the process of extinction — the finding that a conditioned fear response can be weakened, over repeated exposures to the trigger that do not result in the feared outcome, until the pathway's threshold gradually rises back toward where it started. This is not achieved by avoiding the trigger, which tends to preserve the pathway at full strength by never giving the nervous system new evidence to update on. It's achieved specifically by encountering milder versions of the trigger repeatedly, deliberately, in circumstances that allow the nervous system to learn, through direct experience rather than argument, that this particular pattern of signals does not, in fact, reliably predict the catastrophic outcome it once did.

It's worth being specific about the actual timeline over which a pathway strengthens or weakens, because vague reassurance about "healing over time" isn't especially useful without some sense of what's actually happening during that time. Fear-conditioning research, including work building on LeDoux's original findings, suggests the strengthening happens quickly — sometimes after a single sufficiently intense event — while the weakening, through extinction, is typically slower and requires active, repeated, safe exposure rather than passive time alone. This asymmetry matters enormously for how you think about your own history: a single bad afternoon can meaningfully lower your threshold for the next several years, while simply avoiding the subject, hoping the sensitivity fades on its own with the mere passage of time, tends not to work nearly as well as people assume it will. Time alone is not the active ingredient in extinction. Repeated, deliberate, safe re-encounter with a milder version of the trigger is — which is exactly why the overrides in this chapter emphasize planned exposure rather than simply waiting it out.

This is, in a real sense, where every earlier chapter in this book converges. Each of the seven patterns before this one — the red screen, the herd, the story that arrives too late, the wrong kind of fast, the missing floor, the relief that misleads, the expensive round trip — describes a different doorway into the same underlying event: a moment where the alarm fires and the hand moves before the mind finishes catching up. This chapter is where you learn what happens to those doorways after you've walked through one of them. They don't close behind you. They widen, quietly, waiting for the next moment that resembles the last one closely enough to reopen. Which means the real, lasting work of this book was never only about surviving any single panic. It's about what you do in the weeks and months after one, while the pathway is still fresh and unusually easy to strengthen further through repeated, unexamined flight — or, with deliberate attention, unusually available to be gently, safely rewritten instead.

There's a further, relevant layer here from the work of psychiatrist Bessel van der Kolk, whose research on the body's role in storing and re-triggering fear responses found that a genuinely threatening experience doesn't get stored only as an explicit, narratable memory — a story you can tell about what happened. It also gets stored as a bodily, procedural memory, accessible through physical sensation and bypassing conscious recall almost entirely, which is part of why a person can feel the full intensity of an old threat response without being able to say, in the moment, exactly what it's connected to. Van der Kolk's research, developed primarily in the context of more severe trauma, describes a body that "keeps the score" independently of what the conscious mind remembers or has processed. This maps directly onto the teenager's inherited pathway: she doesn't necessarily carry a clear, explicit memory of the specific afternoon her parents panicked. What she carries, more precisely, is a bodily calibration — formed during a period of real household tension — that fires faster and harder than her own direct financial history would predict, because the body doing the calibrating was younger, more impressionable, and simply present in the room. This is not a reason for alarm. It's a reason for patience with yourself specifically in cases where a fast, intense reaction doesn't seem to match anything you can consciously point to — the mismatch itself is data, not evidence that the reaction is fake or exaggerated.

What it costs you

The direct cost is a widening mismatch, over time, between the intensity of your financial reactions and the actual severity of what's triggering them — meaning each subsequent panic-driven decision is increasingly likely to be a significant overreaction to a genuinely modest situation, simply because the pathway has been strengthened past the point of matching the current, milder reality. This tends to compound financially in a specific way: minor, unremarkable market movements, the kind that happen constantly and mean very little on their own, start to reliably trigger the same drastic responses that were, arguably, more defensible during the original, larger event.

The quieter cost is what this does to a person's confidence in their own emotional stability over time, particularly once the pattern becomes visible to people close to them, as it did for the business owner and her partner. Noticing that you go from calm to catastrophic faster and faster, over smaller and smaller triggers, without understanding why, tends to generate a secondary layer of anxiety on top of the original one — a fear of your own reactions, a sense that you can't fully trust your own responses under pressure — which is its own genuine cost, separate from whatever the original financial pattern was doing to your accounts.

There's a third cost worth naming, specific to the compounding nature of sensitization across an entire financial lifetime rather than any single episode: because each unexamined panic widens the pathway further, the years in which a person can least afford repeated panic-driven losses — later in life, closer to or inside retirement, with less time remaining for a portfolio to recover from a badly timed decision — are frequently the same years in which the pathway, after decades of intermittent reinforcement, has become fastest and most sensitive. This is a cruel piece of timing that sensitization research would predict but that rarely gets named plainly: the version of you with the least room for financial error is very often facing the version of your nervous system most primed to produce one, unless the pattern has been deliberately interrupted somewhere along the way.

There's a fourth, more hopeful side to this same compounding pattern worth naming, because sensitization research doesn't only compound in the harmful direction. Just as an unexamined pathway widens further with each unexamined repetition, a pathway that's been deliberately, safely re-encountered — through the kind of planned, low-stakes exposure this chapter's Move describes — narrows measurably with each safe repetition too. The compounding runs both ways. A person who has done the work of gently walking the same road several times, on their own terms, at moments they chose rather than moments that ambushed them, tends to arrive at the years when financial stability matters most with a threshold that has moved back toward normal, rather than one that's been left to widen, untouched, for decades. The same asymmetry that makes this pattern dangerous when ignored is what makes it genuinely correctable when it isn't.

The overrides

Notice the mismatch between the trigger's size and your response's size, explicitly, each time. After any strong financial reaction, ask directly: was the actual situation this severe, or does my response feel more like the last time something like this happened? Naming this gap doesn't eliminate it, but it starts to build the specific kind of awareness that sensitization otherwise operates entirely without — because sensitized responses feel, from the inside, perfectly proportionate to the current threat, and only a deliberate comparison against the actual current facts reveals the mismatch.

The Move: build planned, low-stakes exposure to smaller versions of your trigger, deliberately, rather than avoiding all reminders of it. If a specific kind of financial event — a certain size of drop, a certain kind of headline, a certain kind of client friction — reliably triggers a disproportionate response, deliberately expose yourself to milder, safer versions of that trigger on your own terms, ideally with support, rather than only encountering it unpredictably and at full intensity. Review a modest, expected market dip calmly and on a schedule, rather than only ever encountering downturns as sudden emergencies. This mirrors the extinction process directly: repeated, safe encounters with a milder version of the trigger are what actually lower the threshold back down, not avoidance, and not willpower applied in the moment of the next full-intensity trigger.

Separate the current situation from the memory it's activating, in writing, when the intensity feels

disproportionate. When a reaction feels larger than the current facts seem to justify, write two short lists side by side: what's actually happening right now, and what happened during the original event this might be echoing. Seeing the two side by side, in specific, concrete language, helps the slower, reasoning parts of the brain recognize the mismatch the fast system can't detect on its own — because the fast system isn't comparing severity levels. It's just matching patterns, and it needs help distinguishing a genuine repeat from a rough resemblance.

Get help building new evidence if the pattern isn't loosening on its own. If a strong, sensitized response keeps recurring despite genuine effort to interrupt it, working with a professional experienced in anxiety and fear-based responses — not exclusively a financial professional — is a legitimate, often necessary step, not a sign that the earlier overrides in this book have failed. Sensitized fear pathways, particularly ones rooted in a genuinely frightening original event, sometimes need more structured support to loosen than self-directed practice alone can provide, and seeking that support is itself an act of the same clear-eyed self-management this whole book has been arguing for.

Consider whether your fastest reactions were built by your own history or inherited from someone else's. If a financial fear response feels disproportionate to anything in your own direct experience, ask honestly whether you were present for, or close to, someone else's financial panic earlier in life — a parent, a household, a formative early job — before you had the context to process it as anything other than a general, undifferentiated emergency. Recognizing an inherited pathway doesn't dissolve it instantly, but it does correct a common, unhelpful conclusion people draw about themselves: that a mismatched, oversized reaction with no matching personal history must mean something is wrong with them specifically, rather than simply meaning the pathway has a source outside their own direct experience.

Track your threshold over time, the way you'd track any other slow-moving health indicator. Because sensitization and extinction both compound gradually, a single good or bad episode tells you very little about the overall trend. Keep a simple, ongoing record — even just a few lines after each strong financial reaction, noting the size of the trigger and the intensity of your response — and review it every few months. This turns an invisible, slow-moving pattern into something you can actually observe changing, in either direction, which is often the difference between noticing a widening pathway early enough to interrupt it and only discovering it years later, at the exact moment described above when the stakes are highest and the room for error is smallest.

A panic you survive once doesn't just end — it leaves a faster road behind it. The way back to a normal threshold isn't avoiding that road. It's walking it again, deliberately, at a pace slow enough to prove to yourself it doesn't lead where it used to.

Before You Go

You started this book somewhere in the middle of a feeling — maybe an old memory of a moment you sold too fast, maybe a live, current dread about what you'll do the next time a number moves the wrong way. Either way, you now have something you didn't have before: a specific map of exactly where that feeling comes from, and exactly how many separate places it can be interrupted before it turns into an action you can't take back.

Think back, for a moment, to the people who opened this book: the woman at her kitchen table, watching a red number get redder. The young man reading a headline about a company he'd never held. The retired couple watching a slow decline cross some threshold neither of them had consciously set. The young father, absorbing a fear that wasn't originally his, over a phone call from a rattled relative. None of them were careless. None of them were uninformed. Each of them had, somewhere inside them, everything they needed to make a calmer, better-timed decision — and none of that knowledge was available to them in the specific ninety seconds or four minutes or single afternoon when it actually mattered, because the part of the brain holding that knowledge was not the part running the show. If you recognized yourself in any of them while reading, that recognition is not a diagnosis of a flaw. It's the most useful thing this book can hand you: proof that the pattern is common, mechanical, and predictable enough to have a shape at all — which means it's specific enough to interrupt, one small, pre-built rule at a time.

It's worth saying plainly, one more time, what this book has not tried to do. It hasn't tried to convince you that fear is irrational, or that a well-informed person shouldn't feel anything when an account they've built for years drops sharply in value. That feeling is not a malfunction. It's the oldest, most reliable piece of machinery you own, doing exactly what it evolved to do — scanning for danger, reacting fast, prioritizing survival over accuracy — applied, in this one narrow context, to a kind of danger it was never built to correctly evaluate. You are not broken because a red number on a screen makes your stomach drop. You are, in that moment, exactly as functional as a human being has ever been. The alarm working is not the problem. The alarm being the only voice in the room, with no gap wide enough for a second opinion to arrive before your hand moves, is the problem — and that problem, unlike the alarm itself, is genuinely, practically addressable.

Every override across these chapters has aimed at the same narrow target: not silencing the alarm, which can't be done, but widening the space between the alarm ringing and your hand moving. A written rule made in advance. A delay you committed to before you needed it. A question you ask yourself in the specific moment everything in you is telling you there's no time to ask questions. None of these are complicated. None of them require you to become a fundamentally different, calmer person than the one who opened this book. They only require you to have already decided, in a quiet moment like this one, what the calmer version of you would want the panicked version of you to do — and then to have written it down somewhere the panicked version can actually find it, because in the moment itself, that version of you will not be capable of constructing a good plan from scratch. That's not a criticism. It's the entire point of everything you've just read. The plan has to be built now, by the version of you reading calmly, for the benefit of a version of you who, on some future difficult day, will not be able to build one.

You will still feel the jolt the next time a number falls hard and fast. You will still, at least sometimes, feel the pull of watching other people run, the itch of a story arriving to explain a decision you haven't actually made yet, the vertigo of not knowing where a floor is, the relief that whispers "you did the right thing" the second an irreversible action is taken. None of that goes away because you read a book, and any book that promised you it would be lying to you in exactly the way this one has tried hard not to. What can change — what these chapters were actually built to change — is what happens in the gap between that first jolt and whatever comes next. That gap is small right now, for most people, close to nonexistent, which is exactly why panic-selling feels less like a decision and more like something that simply happens to you. The work of this book has been to make that gap wider, one deliberate rule and one honest naming at a time, until there's enough room inside it for the slower, wiser, more complete version of your thinking to get a seat at the table before anything gets sold, listed, or liquidated that didn't need to be.

If there's one thing worth carrying forward above everything else, let it be this: the instinct to flee was never a character flaw, and it was never evidence that you're bad with money, or bad under pressure, or somehow less disciplined than people who seem to stay calm. It's a perfectly functional piece of ancient machinery, doing its job with total conviction, applied to a threat it can't accurately size up on its own. You don't need to defeat it. You need to build enough structure around it — in advance, in writing, before the alarm rings — that its verdict stops being the only one in the room. That's a realistic goal. It's also, as it turns out, almost the entire difference between a financial life repeatedly wrecked by fear and one that simply, honestly, includes fear as one weather pattern among many, survivable every time, because you built the shelter before the storm arrived rather than during it.

There's one more thing worth saying about how this book hopes to be used over time, rather than just once. The specific triggers described here — a red screen, a crowd's visible fear, a story arriving too fast, a fast-thinking instinct misapplied, an open-ended decline, a wave of premature relief, a costly return trip, a widened pathway — will not stop appearing in your financial life simply because you've now read a clear account of how each one works. They'll keep showing up, on their own schedule, at moments you don't get to choose. What's different, if any of this has actually landed, is that you'll have a name for what's happening while it's happening, not only afterward, in the reconstructed story your mind builds once the moment has passed. A named pattern is a pattern you can catch mid-motion. An unnamed one only becomes visible in hindsight, which is exactly one chapter too late to matter.

One last practical note, since this book has tried throughout to be useful rather than merely comforting: you do not need to implement every override in every chapter today. Pick one. The written-reason habit from Chapter 4, or the mandatory delay from Chapter 2, or the pre-committed re-entry plan from Chapter 8 — whichever one, reading back through these chapters, made you nod in recognition rather than simply follow along. Build that one piece of structure this week, while you're calm, in the specific place you'll actually encounter it again: a note in the app itself, a rule taped somewhere you'll see it, a conversation with whoever shares your financial decisions. The rest of the overrides will still be here, waiting, the next time a chapter's specific trigger shows up in your own life and you find yourself wanting a sturdier answer than the one you have. This isn't a book meant to be fully absorbed and then set aside. It's meant to be returned to, chapter by chapter, exactly when the pattern it describes starts happening to you in real time — which is the only moment any of this was ever actually going to be useful.

Go build your gap. The next alarm is not a question of if. It's only a question of whether, this time, something you put in place today gets a chance to answer it before your hand does.

Notes & Further Reading

The psychological and behavioral-finance concepts referenced throughout this book draw on established, verifiable research. Readers interested in going deeper are pointed toward the original sources and researchers credited in each chapter, rather than toward secondary summaries.

On the neuroscience of threat response and fear conditioning: Joseph LeDoux's research on the amygdala and the fast, subcortical "low road" pathway for threat processing is documented across his body of work, including his influential writing on the emotional brain and the neuroscience of fear and anxiety. His research on fear conditioning and extinction — the process by which conditioned fear responses can be weakened through repeated, safe exposure — underlies the discussion in Chapter 9.

On bodily signals in decision-making: Neuroscientist Antonio Damasio's somatic marker hypothesis, developed through his research on patients with damage to brain regions integrating emotion and decision-making, underlies the discussion in Chapter 1 of how felt, bodily signals shape judgment before conscious reasoning engages.

On affective primacy and the affect heuristic: Robert Zajonc's research on the primacy of affect — the finding that emotional reactions can precede and shape conscious cognitive appraisal — is foundational to the discussion in Chapter 2. The affect heuristic, as studied by Paul Slovic and colleagues working within the broader tradition established by Daniel Kahneman and Amos Tversky, describes the substitution of feeling-based judgments for more effortful evidence-based ones.

On subliminal fear response speed: Neuroscientist Elizabeth Phelps's research on how quickly emotionally significant visual stimuli can trigger amygdala activation and physiological fear responses, often below the threshold of conscious recognition, adds further support to the discussion of pre-verbal reaction speed in Chapter 2.

On judgment under uncertainty and dual-process thinking: Daniel Kahneman and Amos Tversky's foundational research on heuristics and biases, and Kahneman's later synthesis of System 1 (fast, automatic) and System 2 (slow, deliberate) thinking, underlie the discussion in Chapters 4 and 5. Their broader body of work on prospect theory and loss aversion is the well-established backdrop against which this book's narrower focus — the acute, event-triggered flee impulse — is distinguished.

On informational cascades and market psychology: Robert Shiller's research on speculative bubbles, herd behavior, and market psychology, including his writing on irrational exuberance, informs the discussion of social contagion in Chapter 3. Solomon Asch's classic experiments on social conformity, and psychologist Irving Janis's research on groupthink in high-stakes group decision-making, further inform the discussion of cascades in Chapter 3.

On stress appraisal and intolerance of uncertainty: Richard Lazarus's appraisal theory of stress and coping, developed across decades of research into how perceived controllability and predictability shape emotional response to threat, underlies the discussion in Chapter 6. The broader research literature on intolerance of uncertainty as a vulnerability factor in anxiety supports the same discussion.

On investor behavior and the behavior gap: Research into individual investor trading patterns, including work associated with economist Terrance Odean on the timing and outcomes of individual investor decisions, informs the discussion of the behavior gap in Chapter 8.

On expert intuition and recognition-primed decision-making: Psychologist Gary Klein's research on how experts make fast, accurate decisions under genuine time pressure — developed through studies of firefighters, emergency clinicians, and military commanders — informs the discussion in Chapter 5 of when fast thinking can and cannot be trusted.

On risk versus true uncertainty: Economist Frank Knight drew an influential early distinction between quantifiable risk and genuine, unquantifiable uncertainty. That distinction underlies the discussion in Chapter 6 of why statistical reassurance about long-term market recovery doesn't fully resolve the felt sense of an open-ended threat.

On visceral factors and affective forecasting: Economist George Loewenstein's research on how intense emotional and physiological states distort decision-making, and on the broader difficulty of predicting one's own future feelings, informs the discussion of relief-driven urgency in Chapter 7.

On the disposition effect: Researchers Hersh Shefrin and Meir Statman's work identifying the tendency to sell winners early and hold losers too long, anchored to reference-dependent thinking, informs the discussion of re-entry anchoring in Chapter 8.

On the body's role in storing fear responses: Psychiatrist Bessel van der Kolk's research on how threatening experience is stored as bodily, procedural memory in addition to explicit narrative memory informs the discussion of inherited and secondhand fear pathways in Chapter 9.

On negative reinforcement and relief: The behavioral psychology concept of negative reinforcement — the strengthening of a behavior through the removal of an aversive state — is a long-established principle in the field, underlying the discussion of relief-driven decision-making in Chapter 7.

This book does not cite any statistic, study, or survey not directly attributable to a named researcher or well-established body of research. Where a mechanism is described without a specific citation, it reflects general, widely-accepted psychological principles rather than a single study, and readers are encouraged to consult the primary sources above for the full depth of the underlying research.

This book is not financial advice. It does not recommend any specific investment, account, platform, or allocation strategy, and nothing in it should be treated as a substitute for guidance from a qualified financial professional familiar with your specific circumstances. Its subject is behavioral: the psychology of the impulse to flee under financial threat, not the question of what you should actually hold, sell, or buy.

About

The Panic Instinct is part of a library exploring the wired-in patterns that shape how people relate to money — not as a series of character flaws to overcome through willpower, but as a set of honest, researched mechanisms built into every human nervous system, worth understanding on their own terms. Each book in the library isolates one distinct pattern, traces it to its real psychological roots, and offers concrete, decision-level ways to work with it rather than against it.

Every book in this library is built the same way: one pattern, traced honestly to real research, translated into overrides you can actually use under pressure rather than only in hindsight. None of them promise to remove the pattern they describe. All of them are trying to do the one thing that actually holds up under real conditions — widen the gap between the moment the pattern fires and the moment you act on it, until there's room in that gap for the calmer, more complete version of you to have a say.

None of these books ask you to become a different kind of person. They ask you to notice, honestly and without judgment, which specific pattern tends to run the show when the pressure arrives — and then to build one small, concrete piece of structure around that specific pattern, in advance, while you're calm enough to build it well. That's the entire method, repeated across every pattern this library covers. It isn't dramatic. It doesn't promise transformation. It just quietly works, one widened gap at a time, which turns out to be exactly the kind of unglamorous, durable progress that actually holds up on the days that matter most.

If this book helped you recognize the shape of your own alarm a little sooner, the next useful step is simple: notice it again, next time, before it finishes deciding for you. That's the whole practice. It doesn't get more complicated than that, and it doesn't need to.

Also in the Series

Every book in The Money Instinct library stands on its own — read them in any order. If this one was useful, the library continues:

The Money Instinct

The Secrecy Instinct

The Underearning Instinct

The Shame Instinct

The Merge Instinct

The Ceiling Instinct

The Windfall Instinct

The Control Instinct

The Legacy Instinct

The Comparison Instinct

The Enabling Instinct

The Austerity Instinct

The Paralysis Instinct

The Retirement Instinct

The Divorce Instinct

The Enough Instinct

The Overconfidence Instinct

The Vigilance Instinct

The Generosity Instinct